"Pope Francis has made reform of the Church a signature of his pontificate, and Rocco D'Ambrosio has provided adept institutional analysis to shed light on the momentum and challenges inherent in such a bold pursuit. All who care deeply about the outcome and want to understand the context, commitment, and countervailing forces at hand would do well to read this book."

> —Kerry Alys Robinson
> Founding Executive Director and Global Ambassador
> Leadership Roundtable

"Rocco D'Ambrosio argues persuasively that Pope Francis is offering more than just a new leadership style. D'Ambrosio's background in sociology and institutional analysis presents fresh insights into the character of Francis's reformist program and invites hope that this papacy may bring enduring and systemic change to the church."

> —Richard Gaillardetz
> Joseph Professor of Catholic Systematic Theology
> Boston College

"In order to understand Pope Francis's pontificate we need theological analysis as well as an analysis of Francis's approach to Church reform from an institutional-systemic point of view. This book by D'Ambrosio offers a very necessary insider look at the politics of Francis's reform and, most important, of the opposition to Francis."

> —Dr. Massimo Faggioli
> Professor of Historical Theology
> Villanova University

"D'Ambrosio's analysis, by exploring the insights of the human sciences, is enriched by angles of consideration that an exclusively theological vision would be unable to offer. The result is a sharp and coherent study that, like Francis's own style, calls us to mercy but does not justify or tolerate unethical or harmful behavior. To this end, D'Ambrosio's style is transparent and simple, rooted in the conviction that no change is possible without revealing the ugliness and its mechanisms hidden within the reality of the church."

—Emilia Palladino
Civiltà Cattolica

"In this quick read of some one hundred pages, priest-sociologist Rocco D'Ambrosio prompts our discussion about the challenge of the church reform championed by the Pontificate of Pope Francis as it steers a new course, away from the Church's traditional anchor points within Europe; new waters run deep and the cross-currents are hard to navigate. D'Ambrosio brings focus to Francis the person, Francis the reformer, and Francis the pope. The writer's narrative then moves to appraise the general backdrop of the church's institutional components—their rationale and foundation—against which Francis is now pitching his energies."

—Jay Kettle-Williams
editor of diocesan magazine of Portsmouth (UK)

Will Pope Francis Pull It Off?

The Challenge of Church Reform

Rocco D'Ambrosio

Translated by
Barry Hudock

LITURGICAL PRESS
Collegeville, Minnesota

www.litpress.org

Originally published in Italian as *Ce la fara' Francesco? La sfida della riforma ecclesiale* by Edizioni la Meridiana © 2016.

Cover design by Ann Blattner. Photo courtesy of Wikimedia Commons.

Excerpts from documents of the Second Vatican Council are from *Vatican Council II: Constitutions, Decrees, Declarations; The Basic Sixteen Documents*, edited by Austin Flannery, OP, © 1996. Used with permission of Liturgical Press, Collegeville, Minnesota.

1   2   3   4   5   6   7   8   9

Library of Congress Cataloging-in-Publication Data

Names: D'Ambrosio, Rocco, 1963– author.
Title: Will Pope Francis pull it off? : the challenge of church reform / Rocco D'Ambrosio ; translated by Barry Hudock.
Other titles: Ce la farà Francesco. English
Description: Collegeville, Minnesota : Liturgical Press, 2017. | Includes bibliographical references.
Identifiers: LCCN 2016048936 (print) | LCCN 2017003805 (ebook) | ISBN 9780814645017 | ISBN 9780814645260 (ebook)
Subjects: LCSH: Francis, Pope, 1936– | Church renewal—Catholic Church—History—21st century.
Classification: LCC BX1378.7 .D3613 2017 (print) | LCC BX1378.7 (ebook) | DDC 282.09/0512—dc23
LC record available at https://lccn.loc.gov/2016048936

Contents

Acknowledgments

The reflections presented here are the fruit of a personal journey that includes research, study, and sincere engagement with many students and colleagues at the Gregorian University, in the Church of Bari, and at institutions where I am involved as priest and teacher. To these I add, with sincere joy and much gratitude, the schools of formation for social and political engagement organized by Cercasi un Fine (www.cercasiunfine.it). This organization is, for me, not only an extension of my academic endeavors but also a source of valuable insight into the civil, political, and ecclesial realities of Italy. My gratitude also goes to Giuseppe Ferrara, Antonella Piccinin, Pasquale Larocca, Annalisa Pisu, Paola De Filippis, Giovanni Parillo, and Antonio Ciaula for all they have done to help bring this text to fruition.

For the English edition, I am grateful to Gerard Mannion, Juliana and Gary Dellapa, Jay and Rosina Kettle-Williams, Angela Rinaldi, and Nicholas Cachia. The English edition bears only very small differences from the Italian. Some marginal references to the Italian social and ecclesial situation are excluded, and a few short paragraphs were added in the second and seventh chapters. I offer my thanks also to the English translator and, of course, to all of you readers.

September 10, 2016

Introduction

S ince the election of Jorge Mario Bergoglio as bishop of Rome on March 13, 2013, his pontificate has prompted many questions. Perhaps one of the most persistent is: *Will Pope Francis pull it off?*

It is a question asked by believers and nonbelievers alike, interested in understanding the challenges that this pope faces and the results of his response to them. Some observers—those who hope the pope will inspire within the Catholic Church the energy and wisdom necessary to address the challenges of our day—ask it with anxiety and concern. Others ask it through taut lips, with skepticism and opposition, as if to insist that nothing will change, *despite* Pope Francis's misguided efforts. The question is posed by many people, in many ways, and with many answers. Everyone's response is shaped by who they are, how they think, and what they do.

In this little book, I will consider the question and seek answers in light of my own research and professional expertise. I work in the field of institutional analysis, concentrating on the philosophical aspects of the topic. A summary of my thinking is found in two texts: *Come pensano e agiscono le istituzioni* [How Institutions Think and Act] (2011) and *Il potere e chi lo detiene* [Power and Those Who Hold It] (2008). Based on my studies, I propose to offer here an institutional analysis of the Catholic Church in the Bergoglio pontificate. This is not a simple task, but its scope is limited. The difficulty increases when we recall that, as I will explain later, there is considerable resistance on the part of many to investigating and discussing the anthropological and institutional aspects of the life of the church.

Like all knowledge, the answer to our question cannot be reached in an individualistic and isolated manner. The question can (and must) respond to the concerns and perspectives of many: simple faithful, priests and bishops, nonbelievers, theologians, sociologists, psychologists, and more. Each response is worthwhile to the extent that it is the result of reflection and study and that it helps shed light on this complex phenomenon, as all modern phenomena are.

Will Pope Francis pull it off? I shall articulate my response starting with Francis himself and his arrival on the global ecclesial scene, bringing with him a project of reform that is inspired strongly by Vatican II. Then I will address the institutional aspects of the Christian community, its drift into a simplistic ideology, the question of power and corruption, and the appearance of certain scandals. Finally, I will close by considering the prospects of the ongoing reform.

Chapter 1

Papal Politics

Aristotle taught that the person who draws others to form a political community is the greatest of benefactors, because he is able to bring people to build a virtuous and happy life together.[1] Extending this Aristotelian principle, we might say that not only the founder of the community but also the one who reforms and renews it, helping it to grow in goodness, is a great benefactor of the people.

There is no institutional reform project, neither in the church nor in the world, that is not in some way bound to the person who conceives of it, introduces it, and carries it out. Certainly, reform is never the task of a single individual. But the physical, emotional, and intellectual burdens that reform demands of a particular leader are always significant. In the Catholic Church today, that leader is Pope Francis, whose persona, like those of all authentic leaders of reform, plays a considerable part in the project.

It is universally acknowledged that Pope Francis is one of the most highly respected figures in the world today, not only within the Catholic Church, but also outside it. Herein lies the first trap: the reputation and charisma of the leader

---

[1] Aristotle, *Politics*, book 1, section 1253. Available at http://www.perseus.tufts.edu/hopper/text?doc=Perseus%3atext%3a1999.01.0058.

may be overshadowing the message he wishes to transmit and the work he is undertaking.

By way of analogy, it is not unlike the dynamic we sometimes see among adolescents, in which being the fan of a particular musician is more related to the singer's personality than to the songs she sings. You remember little of the songs but carry deep and precise memories of the singer and the emotions she aroused in you. Emotional data has completely dominated and absorbed cognitive data.

Wisdom tells us that emotions and ideas should always be integrated and governed. In Christian terms, they should be subject to discernment.

Pope Francis seems to be well aware of the risk involved in his personal popularity. In an interview with the Italian newspaper *Corriere della Sera*, just a year after his election, he said, "Sigmund Freud said, if I'm not mistaken, that in all idealization there is an aggression. To paint the Pope as if he is a sort of Superman, a sort of star, I find offensive. The Pope is a man who laughs, cries, sleeps peacefully and has friends like everyone else. He is a normal person."[2] In another interview, with the Vatican correspondent Andrea Tornielli, Francis has identified himself as, first of all, "a man who needs the mercy of God."[3]

The pope's comments point to the most obvious mistakes of some of his strongest supporters: mythologizing him; boundless confidence in his reform; excessive expectations from his pontificate; superficial simplifications of ecclesial processes, often expressed with a banal "Francis is here now, he'll do the thinking for us" sort of approach; and a lack of objectivity and

---

[2] "English Translation of Pope Francis' *Corriere della Sera* Interview," Zenit, March 5, 2014: https://zenit.org/articles/english-translation -of-pope-francis-corriere-della-sera-interview/.

[3] Francis, *The Name of God Is Mercy: A Conversation with Andrea Tornielli*, trans. Oonagh Stransky (New York: Random House, 2016), 41.

detachment when assessing his words and actions. Leaders, Francis insisted in an address to the Roman Curia, are not to be "deified." Such idolization can disguise a very real syndrome:

> This is the disease of those who court their superiors in the hope of gaining their favour. They are victims of careerism and opportunism; they honour persons and not God (cf. *Mt* 23:8-12). They serve thinking only of what they can get and not of what they should give.[4]

Francis's references to himself, then, are usually invitations to look at his gestures and to listen to his teaching with much more balance, avoiding fanaticism and harmful mythologization.

Will Pope Francis pull it off? He will to the extent that we can avoid fanaticism and mythologizing. This means in practical terms to focus more on what he says and does and less on who he is.

On the opposite side, there are those who refuse to accept him and often denigrate him. At the beginning of the pontificate, these critics seemed to voice their objections quietly, but they have more recently come confidently into the open. A quick review of a few websites immediately reveals an array of fierce criticism. We find frequent use of expressions like communist, pauperist, doctrinally weak, destroyer of the Church, heretic, ecologist, betrayer of tradition, contrary to Catholic moral teaching on family, inappropriate wardrobe, exaggerated gestures, a Jesuit who wants to be Franciscan, too unfiltered and blunt, reckless, simplistic, undiplomatic, and more.

There is no shortage of books, newspaper articles, and interviews with clergy and lay faithful who criticize various

---

[4] Francis, Presentation of Christmas Greetings to the Roman Curia, December 22, 2014: https://w2.vatican.va/content/francesco/en/speeches/2014/december/documents/papa-francesco_20141222_curia-romana.html.

statements of the pope that they consider unfaithful to Catholic doctrine. In these comments, two aspects are particularly surprising. First, much of this fierce criticism comes from people who have been, with past popes, emphatic about their loyalty to the Supreme Pontiff; their much-heralded fidelity and obedience now seems to have waned. Second, their mind-set resembles those who support ideological regimes: the doctrine/tradition is untouchable; anyone who questions it—let alone attempts philosophical or theological research into it—is a heretic; and the task of pastors and teachers is only to repeat it and defend it, always and everywhere. As far as one can tell from press reports, the last gathering of the Synod of Bishops demonstrated to what extent these two factors can stand in the way of Francis's efforts.

There is also a third group, which could be described as *neither for nor against* Francis. They seem to be favorable to the conciliar nature of the pope's thinking, though they are careful not to say it too publicly; indeed, they say as little as possible about Pope Francis. They like some things about the pope but are annoyed by other things, like his undiplomatic style and frankness, his exaggerated concern for social issues and poverty, and so on. In short, they like the pope, but not enough to say it publicly, and not enough to get involved in his project of reform. Here we encounter subtle sorts of ambiguity and hypocrisy. In a sense, this group is more "dangerous" than the one more openly opposed to the papal reforms.

These groups exist. It would be an exaggeration to regard them as full-fledged "parties," structured and organized, or as schools of thought, able to develop theories distinct from the more formal and prominent ones. They should be considered more as anthropological and ethical *tendencies*, like those present in all institutions, reflecting mostly the thinking of individual members who, in some cases, gather to share their thoughts. In other words, they're a loosely organized group that rarely exists for long, for lack of leadership or vision.

Insofar as these groups contribute to institutional debates in healthy, grounded, and constructive ways, they are positive and helpful phenomena. But when they operate covertly, rejecting any form of dialogue, they become a liability.

To the existence of such factions and intra-ecclesial opposition, Francis responds by insisting on the importance of dialogue, so that the diversity will become a source of enrichment and never a cause for division. His frequent calls for dialogue seem inspired by *Ecclesiam Suam*, Paul VI's programmatic first encyclical released during and itself inspired by the Second Vatican Council. In that document, Pope Paul VI proposed to all Catholics the practice of listening humbly to the world, based on "consideration and esteem for others . . . understanding and . . . kindness" and in a way that rejects "bigotry and prejudice, malicious and indiscriminate hostility, and empty, boastful speech." Such listening seeks always the good of the other party, out of a "desire to respect a man's freedom and dignity," with the aim of "a fuller sharing of ideas and convictions."[5]

Because this kind of dialogue is so demanding and difficult, it is too often easier to approach others—especially those who think differently than us—assertively and closed-mindedly, as modern-day crusaders and ideologists unwilling to meet anyone halfway. The rejection of dialogue is found at almost all levels of the church and just as surely outside the Catholic community, among various Protestant, Jewish, and Muslim communities, not to mention among nonbelievers and others whose ethical, cultural, political, and economic positions are different from ours.

---

[5] Paul VI, Encyclical *Ecclesiam Suam* (On the Church), August 6, 1964, n. 79: http://w2.vatican.va/content/paul-vi/en/encyclicals/documents/hf_p-vi_enc_06081964_ecclesiam.html.

In his homily for the feast of Epiphany in 2016, Francis said,

> The Magi mentioned in the Gospel of Matthew are a living witness to the fact that the seeds of truth are present everywhere, for they are the gift of the Creator, who calls all people to acknowledge him as good and faithful Father. The Magi represent the men and women throughout the world who are welcomed into the house of God. Before Jesus, all divisions of race, language and culture disappear: in that Child, all humanity discovers its unity. The Church has the task of seeing and showing ever more clearly the desire for God which is present in the heart of every man and woman.[6]

The task Francis was pointing to is one that, more often than not, remains incomplete.

---

[6] Francis, Holy Mass on the Solemnity of the Epiphany of the Lord, January 6, 2016: https://w2.vatican.va/content/francesco/en/homilies /2016/documents/papa-francesco_20160106_omelia-epifania.html.

Chapter 2

Nothing New: Just Vatican II

Associates of Yves Congar reported that this great theological architect of Vatican II believed the council would not be fully realized until fifty years after it concluded. If so, we can say that we are living now in that season to which Congar looked with hope.

Pope Francis—as many have observed—can be understood only in the light of Vatican II. He is the first pope who did not participate in the council. Many of the reference points of his thinking and teaching are conciliar. This becomes clear, however, only by a careful and specialized reading of what he says, because his awareness of the council is so assimilated and mature that his references seem on the surface to be his own voice, rather than direct quotations of the council itself. Put simply, Francis often cites the council—without citing it.

It is true that from the doctrinal point of view, the pope's teaching offers nothing new. But we need to dig a bit deeper than that to understand this better. At times the pope's discourses (both written and extemporaneous), his encyclicals and apostolic exhortations, his addresses, his homilies, and his messages seem not so much to be for the purpose of teaching doctrine as to point us toward practices of renewal, to call us to be more faithful to the will of God. This is not to suggest that his magisterium lacks a biblical or theological foundation. This is far from the case. It means, rather, that the doctrinal aspects are in the service of a reform of ecclesial structures and practices. His aim is to make the church more faithful to the Gospel, "to continue," as he put it, "on the journey of the Second Vatican Council and divest ourselves of useless and hurtful things, of false worldly security that weigh down the Church and injure her true face."[1]

In saying "nothing new," therefore, we are referring specifically to doctrine. The same cannot be said about his style and his insistence on the priority of certain themes and issues. With regard to style, we should be clear that every pope—like every person—is who he is "in his unique, unrepeatable human reality," as John Paul II put it.[2] In speaking of Francis's particular style, the point is not simply to draw up a list of personal priorities in descending order of importance but rather to understand his "unique and unrepeatable" characteristics in order to assess their impact on the reform he proposes. This is not to ignore the fact that Francis's thinking and practices are inspired, in particular, by the popes who preceded him. It is undeniable, for example, that in his serene goodness and his wisdom borne of years and experience, we see John XXIII, while his firm rootedness in the council's primary themes recalls the profound theological synthesis of Paul VI. That said, Francis is Francis, with his solid conciliar grounding and his remarkable style of communication.

This reference to his communication style raises another important consideration. What is new about Francis is not merely

---

[1] Francis, Address to Participants in the Plenary of the Pontifical Council for Promoting the New Evangelization, October 14, 2014: https://w2.vatican.va/content/francesco/en/speeches/2013/october /documents/papa-francesco_20131014_plenaria-consiglio-nuova -evangelizzazione.html.

[2] John Paul II, Encyclical *Redemptor Hominis*, March 4, 1979, n. 13: http://w2.vatican.va/content/john-paul-ii/en/encyclicals/documents /hf_jp-ii_enc_04031979_redemptor-hominis.html.

his personal charisma. It is, above all, his insistence on bringing the church ever more fully into modernity, with its whole being and without betraying itself. This was, after all, one of the council's primary aims, as Paul VI expressed so clearly: "Sharing the noblest aspirations of men and suffering when she sees these aspirations not satisfied, she wishes to help them attain their full realization. So she offers man her distinctive contribution: a global perspective on man and human realities."[3]

Francis's church is a church that *helps and proclaims*: it helps people, especially the least ones, and it proclaims the Gospel of the Lord. Francis's church does not command, and it does not impose. Its gestures and its words—at least those of the pope himself—reflect this vision.

Francis touched on the subject of the church and modernity quite specifically as he inaugurated the Jubilee Year of Mercy:

> Today, here in Rome and in all the dioceses of the world, as we pass through the Holy Door, we also want to re-member another door, which fifty years ago the Fathers of the Second Vatican Council opened to the world. This anniversary cannot be remembered only for the legacy of the Council's documents, which testify to a great ad-vance in faith.[4]

The reference to the *open door* recalls a remark that has been attributed to Pope John XXIII but which was in fact made by Cardinal François Marty, the archbishop of Paris, in 1968. He described the context in a 1985 interview:

[3] Paul VI, Encyclical *Populorum Progressio* (On the Development of Peoples), March 26, 1967, n. 13: http://w2.vatican.va/content/paul-vi /en/encyclicals/documents/hf_p-vi_enc_26031967_populorum.html.

[4] Francis, Homily, Holy Mass and Opening of the Holy Door, December 8, 2015: https://w2.vatican.va/content/francesco/en /homilies/2015/documents/papa-francesco_20151208_giubileo -omelia-apertura.html.

In September 1968, I was visited by General De Gaulle, President of the Republic. I had been the archbishop of Paris only for a few months. The events of May were still alive and disturbing in his memory, and he still could not understand why everything had erupted as it had. Suddenly he said to me, "You see, May 1968 is like the collapse of the dam above Fréjus.[5] Nothing can stop the water when a dam gives way. No one has been able to stop May of '68, even General de Gaulle." He added, "I wonder if the Church is about to experience its own Fréjus dam collapse?" I'm not good with quick responses; I come from a family of farmers. So I did not answer immediately. But then a thought occurred to me and I told him: "Mr. President, a few moments ago you were wondering if the Church will have its own Fréjus. But you know, the Church had the Council. . . ." I can still see General de Gaulle turning to me, great as he was, and saying, "You're right. You did, and at the right moment." Well, I think he was right.[6]

To the category of openness to the world, Francis adds the call to encounter. We hear in this the echoes of many themes (not just the one mentioned explicitly here by Francis) that were dear to Paul VI:

Before all else, the Council was an encounter. A genuine *encounter between the Church and the men and women of our time.* An encounter marked by the power of the Spirit, who impelled the Church to emerge from the shoals which for years had kept her self-enclosed so as to set out once again, with enthusiasm, on her missionary

[5] Two historical notes help explain the context. May 1968 was a historically volatile period of civil unrest in France. On December 2, 1959, France's Malpasset Dam ruptured and the resulting torrent of water inundated the nearby town of Fréjus, killing over four hundred people.—Trans.

[6] *Corriere della Sera*, December 15, 1985.

journey. It was the resumption of a journey of encountering people where they live: in their cities and homes, in their workplaces. Wherever there are people, the Church is called to reach out to them and to bring the joy of the Gospel, and the mercy and forgiveness of God. After these decades, we again take up this missionary drive with the same power and enthusiasm. The Jubilee challenges us to this openness, and demands that we not neglect the spirit which emerged from Vatican II, the spirit of the Samaritan, as Blessed Paul VI expressed it at the conclusion of the Council. May our passing through the Holy Door today commit us to making our own the mercy of the Good Samaritan.[7]

With regard to the central themes of this pontificate, it must be said that they have a double origin. On one hand is the personal history of the pope himself and his assimilation of Vatican II; on the other are the concerns and priorities expressed by the College of Cardinals at the time of his election. The pope himself has acknowledged: "The changes also come from two sources: what we Cardinals asked for, and what has to do with my own personality."[8]

To speak of the pope's personality is to refer to Jorge Mario Bergoglio's life journey: understanding the spiritual roots and the personal and ecclesial experiences that have led to the maturity of his understanding of the council. But obviously there is more to Francis's reform than his biographical data; ecclesial reform was a central element of the discussions

---

[7] Francis, Homily, Holy Mass and Opening of the Holy Door, December 8, 2015: https://w2.vatican.va/content/francesco/en/homilies/2015/documents/papa-francesco_20151208_giubileo-omelia-apertura.html.

[8] Francis, Press Conference during the Return Flight from Rio De Janeiro for World Youth Day XXVIII, July 28, 2013: http://w2.vatican.va/content/francesco/en/speeches/2013/july/documents/papa-francesco_20130728_gmg-conferenza-stampa.html.

among the cardinals prior to the papal election, as he himself recalled in July 2013:

> The steps I have taken during these four and a half months come from two sources: the content of what had to be done, all of it, comes from the General Congregations of the Cardinals. There were certain things that we Cardinals asked of the one who was to be the new Pope. I remember that I asked for many things, thinking that it would be someone else.[9]

Given all of this, it is not surprising that Francis has focused so much of his attention on the issue of ecclesial reform. One particular point should be noted. Despite some appearances, the reform is following a precise and strategic plan, of which even the finest details are considered. One day historians will show that nothing has been left to chance: the extemporaneous interviews, the gestures, the legislative and disciplinary measures, the internal and public responses to well-known scandals. They are all—in my opinion—various aspects of a considered plan of action. Together they demonstrate leadership on the part of the pope that is careful and intentional, reflecting developed strategies and aiming toward specific results, all with a good dose of discernment, patience, and understanding. In short, the pope is no fool.

But there is more to consider. Indeed, there are further crucial issues to be addressed. For Francis the reform will only have succeeded if it restores vitality, both theoretical and practical, to issues such as the preferential option for the poor, the church's missionary impulse, poverty and prudence in ecclesial life, the commitment to justice, the fight against corruption within all institutions (including the Catholic Church), the eradication of the scourge of pedophilia, episcopal collegiality, the promotion of the role of the

[9] Ibid.

laity, pastoral attention to family life, a renewed ecumenical commitment, and care for the environment, to mention only the most significant ones.

And not mentioning other issues does not mean he is ignoring them. It could simply mean that he believes these issues do not need as much attention, because they are already clear in doctrine and practice. The answer that Pope Francis gave in a 2013 interview is illuminating:

> We cannot insist only on issues related to abortion, gay marriage and the use of contraceptive methods. This is not possible. I have not spoken much about these things, and I was reprimanded for that. But when we speak about these issues, we have to talk about them in a context. The teaching of the church, for that matter, is clear and I am a son of the church, but it is not necessary to talk about these issues all the time.[10]

But the themes Francis wishes to emphasize are not always welcomed in some sectors of the church. From the institutional point of view, this is nothing new. The more radical, intensive, and broad the reform one wishes to introduce, the stronger the reaction will be. (Vatican II is a case in point.)

Institutions resist innovation. This explains the strong resistance, at this moment, to Francis's reform. The debate over the pope's style, his conception of power, and the eloquent gestures of his ministry are small matters compared to the fact that the institutional church is faced now with a momentous choice: to implement Vatican II (a process that is not yet complete) or return to a previous model of what it means to be the church.

We cannot forget that the election of Francis was preceded by debates in both Europe and North America in which some

[10] Antonio Spadaro, Interview with Pope Francis: https://w2.vatican .va/content/francesco/en/speeches/2013/september/documents /papa-francesco_20130921_intervista-spadaro.html.

called into question the validity of the council itself. Finding ourselves now with a pope who intends to implement it and, further, to reform the church according to the spirit of that council, we should not be surprised to see, among traditionalists and reactionaries, much resistance. It has often seemed, in recent decades, that we have lost that spirit of the council that the bishop of my own Diocese of Bari spoke of when he returned from the experience, feeling "new, renewed in the spirit of the council," an event that he believed "calls upon our whole selves, totally, calling us to an absolute commitment, without reserve."[11]

To be renewed by the council, not only personally and communally, but institutionally, we must call into question a widely accepted model of the church. I refer to the sort of church that seems to have many certainties and few doubts, that insists on giving attention to certain moral issues while neglecting others, that seeks the numerical majority and cultural preeminence, that demands privileges and subsidies from the state, that ignores corruption and the misuse of power, that is clericalized and very hierarchically organized, and that does little to promote the laity.

In this model of the church, there is little room for the themes and issues that are so central to Francis's pontificate. Francis himself articulated these themes to the United States bishops in these words:

> The innocent victim of abortion, children who die of hunger or from bombings, immigrants who drown in the search for a better tomorrow, the elderly or the sick who are considered a burden, the victims of terrorism, wars, violence and drug trafficking, the environment

---

[11] E. Nicodemo, "Nota redazionale: Il ritorno dell'arcivescovo dal Concilio," in *L'Odegitria: Bollettino Ecclesiastico ufficiale per l'Archidiocesi di Bari* (1965), 12, pp. 405–9, at 407.

devastated by man's predatory relationship with nature—at stake in all of this is the gift of God, of which we
are noble stewards but not masters. It is wrong, then, to
look the other way or to remain silent. No less important
is the Gospel of the Family, which in the World Meeting
of Families in Philadelphia I will emphatically proclaim
together with you and the entire Church.[12]

More briefly, in an interview with the Argentine newspaper *La Voz del Pueblo*, he identified as the greatest evils of
the world as "poverty, corruption, and human trafficking."[13]

For many in the church, assimilating these priorities requires a radical change of mind-set or, as the pope has put it,
putting aside some established plans. He writes in *Evangelii
Gaudium*:

> God's word is unpredictable in its power. The Gospel
> speaks of a seed which, once planted, grows by itself,
> even while the farmer sleeps (Mk 4:26-29). The Church
> must accept this uncontrollable freedom of the Word,
> which accomplishes what it wills in ways that often sur-
> pass our calculations and wreak havoc upon our plans.[14]

---

[12] Francis, Meeting with the Bishops of the United States of America,
September 23, 2015: https://w2.vatican.va/content/francesco/en
/speeches/2015/september/documents/papa-francesco_20150923
_usa-vescovi.html.

[13] "Añoro ir a una pizzería y comerme una buena pizza," La
Voz del Pueblo, May 31, 2015: http://www.lavozdelpueblo.com.ar
/nota-27095--aoro-ir-a-una-pizzera-y-comerme-una-buena-pizza.

[14] Francis, Apostolic Exhortation *Evangelii Gaudium* (On the Proclamation of the Gospel in Today's World), November 24, 2013, n. 22. (My
translation. The phrase that the author will draw attention to in this
and the following two quoted passages—"rompere i nostri schemi," to
wreak havoc upon our plans [or more colloquially: to throw a monkey
wrench into our plans]—is identical in the Italian of each but has been
translated with some variety ["to surpass our ways of thinking," "to
wreak havoc with our plans," "to break molds"] in the Vatican's English

In fact, the idea of "wreaking havoc upon our plans" comes up often in Francis's teaching. It is more than a call to accept the task of ecclesial reform; rather, it is a clear conviction of faith. Among many additional references from his words, I cite only two others:

> "God constantly surprises us. He bursts our categories. He wreaks havoc upon our plans."[15]

> "God . . . wreaks havoc upon one's plans. Unless we have the courage to ignore our own plans, we will never go forward because our God pushes us to do this: to be creative about the future."[16]

The emphasis is on the disruption of plans. To understand it, there is no need to point to political parties, factions, or defections. One needs only to accept Vatican II as a point of no return for the Catholic Church on its journey through history. Vatican II, Francis has said,

> produced a renewal movement that simply comes from the same Gospel. Its fruits are enormous. Just recall the liturgy. The work of liturgical reform has been a service to the people as a re-reading of the Gospel from a concrete historical situation. Yes, there are hermeneutics of continuity and discontinuity, but one thing is clear: the

---

translations. In order to make the author's point clear and avoid confusion for the reader, the translations of these three passages provided here are my own.—Trans.)

[15] Francis, Holy Mass for the Marian Day on the Occasion of the Year of Faith, October 13, 2013: http://w2.vatican.va/content/francesco/en/homilies/2013/documents/papa-francesco_20131013_omelia-giornata-mariana.html.

[16] Francis, Meeting with the World of Labour and Industry, July 5, 2014: https://w2.vatican.va/content/francesco/en/speeches/2014/july/documents/papa-francesco_20140705_molise-mondo-del-lavoro.html.

dynamic of reading the Gospel, actualizing its message for today—which was typical of Vatican II—is absolutely irreversible.[17]

This rereading of the Gospel, carried out by Vatican II, is therefore the criterion by which this pontificate may be evaluated. Those who accept only a preconciliar model of Christian life and of the church will deem Francis's reform, in various instances, to be heretical, unfounded, inadequate, and so on. Those who embrace the council's reading of the Gospel will seek to evaluate the reform primarily by the principles it articulates and the ways they are put into practice, rather than by focusing on the person of the pope, who, like every human being and any leader, however gifted and wise, occasionally makes mistakes.

Regarding the pope's personal limitations and more broadly his implementation of the reform, we can recognize three fundamental attitudes, each of which will be addressed in the pages that follow. In short, these are:

1. An honest and well-founded constructive criticism that aims at supporting and assisting the pope in the work of reform through spiritual and intellectual contributions; through the promotion of new ecclesial practices that rest on the specific responsibilities of bishops, priests, religious, and laypeople; and through the strengthening of an ever more authentically conciliar culture within the church.

2. The passive reliance on antiquated and preconciliar models of the church, not even necessarily with evil intentions, but out of a laziness and inertia that are difficult to overcome.

---

[17] Spadaro, "Interview."

3. Opposition to the pope, often forceful and even violent, carried out by people who have little idea what they are causing and the repentance they need to engage in.

And yet the reform, like a large construction site always in progress, moves forward. In a homily during his apostolic visit to the United States, Pope Francis provided a reminder of what a Christian approach to such work ought to look like:

> We can get caught up measuring the value of our apostolic works by the standards of efficiency, good management and outward success which govern the business world. Not that these things are unimportant! We have been entrusted with a great responsibility, and God's people rightly expect accountability from us. But the true worth of our apostolate is measured by the value it has in God's eyes. To see and evaluate things from God's perspective calls for constant conversion in the first days and years of our vocation and, need I say, it calls for great humility. The cross shows us a different way of measuring success. Ours is to plant the seeds: God sees to the fruits of our labors. And if at times our efforts and works seem to fail and produce no fruit, we need to remember that we are followers of Jesus . . . and his life, humanly speaking, ended in failure, in the failure of the cross.[18]

[18] Francis, Vespers with Priests and Religious, September 24, 2015: http://w2.vatican.va/content/francesco/en/homilies/2015/documents/papa-francesco_20150924_usa-omelia-vespri-nyc.html.

Chapter 3

A Church That Is Human
(and More)

Pope Francis is not afraid to deal with the scandals, infidelities, and other problems that face the Catholic Church. He has shared the conviction that guides him in these matters:

> But there will be inconsistencies, they will always be there because we are human, and so reform has to be ongoing. The Fathers of the Church used to say: "Ecclesia semper reformanda." We have to be concerned to reform the Church day by day, because we are sinners, we are weak, and there are going to be problems.[1]

In other words, Francis seeks a reform of the church that is neither wishful thinking, on the one hand, nor a destructive planning, on the other. Here, too, the pope is guided by a conviction of faith: "Jesus not only took away evil, but transformed it into good. He did not change things with words,

---

[1] Francis, Interview with Journalists during the Return Flight from the Holy Land, May 26, 2014: https://w2.vatican.va/content/francesco /en/speeches/2014/may/documents/papa-francesco_20140526_terra -santa-conferenza-stampa.html.

but with deeds; not in appearance, but in substance; not superficially, but radically."[2]

The ongoing reform that Francis seeks obviously aims at the church's human aspects. It is founded on a fundamental belief: the church is an institution that is both human and divine. As a matter of faith, every believer knows that "the church, in Christ, is a sacrament—as a sign and instrument, that is, of communion with God and of the unity of the entire human race."[3] But it is also a human institution composed of men and women who bear both the burden and the beauty of their humanity, all of their own limitations and virtues, the splendor of their holiness and the darkness of their sin. One can extend to the whole Christian community what Francis said to the Roman Curia: "The [Church] is called constantly to improve and to grow in *communion, holiness and wisdom,* in order to carry out fully its mission. And yet, like any body, like any human body, it is also exposed to diseases, malfunctioning, infirmity."[4]

Though all of this may seem obvious, it isn't to everyone. To speak of the human aspects of the church often draws objections. They are practical, certainly not theological. In fact, Catholic tradition has always acknowledged the church's dual nature. Jesus recognized that his disciples were "evil" (Luke 11:13). He rebukes Peter for his sins and asks for confirmation of his loyalty. Augustine said that the church had

---

[2] Francis, Papal Mass for the Repose of the Souls of the Cardinals and Bishops who Died over the Course of the Year, November 3, 2015: https://w2.vatican.va/content/francesco/en/homilies/2015/documents/papa-francesco_20151103_omelia-suffragio-defunti.html.

[3] Second Vatican Council, Dogmatic Constitution on the Church, *Lumen Gentium* 1, in *Vatican Council II: Constitutions, Decrees, Declarations,* ed. Austin Flannery (Collegeville, MN: Liturgical Press, 2014).

[4] Francis, Presentation of the Christmas Greetings to the Roman Curia, December 22, 2014: https://w2.vatican.va/content/francesco/en/speeches/2014/december/documents/papa-francesco_20141222_curia-romana.html.

been "a whore" who "used to go fornicating after idols and demons," until she became "a virgin," made so by "the kindness and mercy of her liberator."[5] Vatican II affirms that "the church, clasping sinners to its bosom, at once holy and always in need of purification, follows constantly the path of penance and renewal."[6]

The church, humanly speaking, is an institution like any other. I have in mind the definition of an institution provided by the great British social anthropologist, Mary Douglas: a "legitimized social grouping." An institution, according to Douglas, may be a family, a game, or a ceremony. Its legitimacy is conferred by a legitimating authority, which recognizes the group, its behavior, and its rules.[7] These rules might be, for example, a constitution, a deeply rooted tradition or cultural practice, an ideology, a widespread feeling, the perceived cosmic order, a religious revelation (as in the case of the church), and so on.

The church, as a religious institution, is one of the *fundamental institutions*. The human sciences recognize certain institutions that are *so universally diffused* that they may be called *fundamental*. Eric Voegelin identifies six: family, work, commerce (today we would say "the market"), culture, religion, and politics.[8] These are the most basic areas in which men and women experience the need to coordinate with one another to establish and implement rules. In a sense they are the *places* (*topoi*) of the institutions, whose symbolic representation is almost universal.

[5] Augustine, Sermon 213, 8, in *Sermons*, trans. Edmund Hill, The Works of Saint Augustine III/6 (New Rochelle, NY: New City Press, 1993), 145.

[6] *Lumen Gentium* 8.

[7] Mary Douglas, *How Institutions Think* (Syracuse: Syracuse University Press, 1986), 46.

[8] Eric Voegelin, *The Nature of Law and Related Legal Writings*, ed. Robert Anthony Pascal, James Lee Babin, and John William Corrington (Baton Rouge: Louisiana State University Press, 1991), 41.

As a legitimized social grouping, the church—as I have said—consists of people, with all the physical, cognitive, and emotional aspects that make up their lives. It is therefore marked by all of the classical anthropological and ethical dynamics: respect for persons and abuse of them, faith and betrayal, aggregation and disintegration, effective leadership and mismanagement, honest use of earthly goods and forms of corruption and violence. This is the reality of the church for all time, starting with the original community described in the Acts of the Apostles, with all its lights and shadows, until the end of days. All of these aspects must be included in any institutional analysis of the Christian community, for a precise reason.

In a famous passage, Thomas Aquinas writes:

> Sacred doctrine makes use even of human reason, not, indeed, to prove faith (for thereby the merit of faith would come to an end), but to make clear other things that are put forward in this doctrine. Since therefore grace does not destroy nature, but perfects it, natural reason should minister to faith as the natural bent of the will ministers to charity.[9]

The richness of this passage requires us to proceed carefully. Subjecting the church to institutional analysis doesn't mean demonstrating its divine nature and the faith that binds us to it; it means, rather, to *make use of reason to clarify* the nature of this community. No one who wants the church to be recognized as authentic can afford either to deny or to hide what Carl Jung would have called its *shadow*.[10] Indeed, we

---

[9] Thomas Aquinas, *Summa Theologica* (New York: Benziger Brothers, 1947), I, q. 1, a. 8 (pp. 5–6).

[10] See, for example, Carl Jung, *Aion*, vol. 9, bk. 2, of *Collected Works of C. G. Jung* (Princeton, NJ: Princeton University Press, 1979), 14; and "On the Psychology of the Unconscious," in *Two Essays on Analytical*

must have the courage to recognize, evaluate, and address it. The very nature of this institution in the plan of God is that it is a people who are in the world but not of the world (John 17). Vito Mignozzi writes, "[In the Church,] the institutional elements are not, in fact, guarantees and assurances for the work of the Spirit, but signs and instruments of it."[11]

Augustine himself, when he speaks of chastity of the church, makes it clear that Christ

> found [the church] a whore [and] he made her a virgin. She mustn't deny that she was once a whore, or she may forget the kindness and mercy of her liberator. How can she not have been a whore, when she used to go fornicating after idols and demons? Fornication of the heart was there in all her members, fornication of the flesh in some of them; of the heart in all.[12]

Lorenzo Milani, the great twentieth-century Italian thinker and pastor, recognizes the gradual growth that must occur from a distorted human nature to full humanity to, finally, the grace of faith: "One can go from being a beast to a person and from a person to a saint. But going from a beast to saint is not possible."[13] Building on Milani's thinking, we can say that an institutional analysis of the church must discern the ways we have been living as beasts, in order to recover a humanity worthy of the name, and so finally to move more authentically toward holiness. "Grace," Thomas said, "perfects nature."

Psychology, vol. 7 of *Collected Works of C. G. Jung* (Princeton, NJ: Princeton University Press, 1972), 35.

[11] Vito Mignozzi, *Come un sacramento. Uno stile per essere Chiesa oggi* (Todi: Tau, 2011), 33.

[12] Augustine, Sermon 213, 8; 145.

[13] Lorenzo Milani, *Esperienze pastorali* (Firenze: Lef, 1957), 326.

Obviously every institutional analysis—including this one—is incomplete, because it stops at anthropological and ethical *reasoning*, rather than going further, toward a complete picture, by taking into consideration the data of faith. In other words, we are following the Thomist way: from nature to grace, which is the perfection of nature itself. In our case, an institutional analysis of the church represents the necessary and indispensable *foundation* for an understanding that is rooted in faith.

We can cite once again the words of Thomas Aquinas, when he speaks of the relationship between the literal sense and the spiritual sense in the interpretation of Scripture: "That signification whereby things signified by words have themselves also a signification is called the spiritual sense, which is based on the literal, and presupposes it."[14] An institutional analysis of the church is the literal sense, and there can be no spiritual sense that doesn't rest on and presuppose the literal sense. In other words, to speak of the church means to refer to all that God has revealed to us about it, but it also means to remember, at the same time, that the church is a human institution.

Pope Francis's words to the Italian church were clear and quite relevant:

> Before the evils or problems of the Church it is useless to seek solutions in conservatism and fundamentalism, in the restoration of obsolete practices and forms that even culturally lack the capacity to be meaningful. Christian doctrine is not a closed system, incapable of raising questions, doubts, inquiries, but is living, is able to unsettle, is able to enliven. It has a face that is supple, a body that moves and develops, flesh that is tender: Christian doctrine is called Jesus Christ.

[14] *Summa Theologica* I, q. 1, a. 10.

The reform of the Church then—and the Church is *semper reformanda*—is foreign to Pelagianism. She is not exhausted in the countless plans to change her structures. It instead means being implanted and rooted in Christ, allowing herself to be led by the Spirit. Thus everything will be possible with genius and creativity.[15]

[15] Francis, Meeting with the Participants in the Fifth Convention of the Italian Church, November 10, 2015: https://w2.vatican.va/content /francesco/en/speeches/2015/november/documents/papa-francesco _20151110_firenze-convegno-chiesa-italiana.html.

Chapter 4

Understanding the Church
without Simplism or Ideology

To adequately understand the life of the church, both institutionally and theologically, there is no place for simplistic or superficial thinking. That we find both is thanks largely to the belief that a basic understanding of institutional dynamics is a matter for specialists. We fail to realize how such ignorance affects us, even on an emotional level. Lacking the tools to understand many problems, they become taboo. We regard them dangerous sources of fear and imbalance. As a result, they become amplified, even pathologically. All institutions, including the church, are complex phenomena; they can be fully understood and evaluated only through careful examination of all that makes them up. Not everyone needs to be a specialist in institutional analysis, but everyone should, for their own good, understand an institution's processes to a degree proportionate to their role in it. In the case of the church, this becomes a duty and a necessity for all pastors and pastoral leaders. In particular, it is important to acquire the tools to help us understand what the human sciences have to teach us. Drawing from them, we can equip ourselves with the basics that will allow us to make a fair assessment of the anthropological and ethical processes that most strongly mark the church's life.

We too often approach and evaluate modernity superficially, too. The nature of "today's world" and all its crises is a recurring theme in our ecclesial discourse: homilies, catechesis, pastoral writings, publications. But it's not easy to talk accurately about the world we live in. The first difficulty lies in always keeping in mind the fact that the contemporary world is a complex reality. Like any complex reality, one needs good tools to see and understand it. In a monolithic culture, one or two "pairs of glasses" are enough to "see" reality; in a more complex culture, we need several more. Any blanket statements about the contemporary world being one thing or another end up being nothing more than trivial and even stupid generalizations.

What world are we talking about? "Today's world," "people," "the contemporary mentality"—such categories are each too broad to mean anything, and we would be wise to avoid them. They say everything and therefore say nothing. In a society that is no longer monolithic, positions and opinions are too many and too diverse for such generalization. Maybe—if I could hazard a guess—that is why Pope Francis prefers to approach issues relating to the contemporary world by starting first with their anthropological aspects, which he then reads in the light of Scripture and church tradition.

More than ever before, we need to study the contemporary context and institutions, including the church, through a combination of disciplines, that is, using tools that draw on different kinds of knowledge to investigate human realities: anthropology, ethics, theology, sociology, psychology, political science, law, economics. No one, including educators and intellectuals, is expected to master *all* of these disciplines— that would be an inconsistent and foolish demand. But what is necessary is an ability to synthesize the information that is available, in order to help and especially to teach others. Making such a synthesis provides one with a map that enables us to find our way through the maze of this world. It also provides a foundation on which one can, if she chooses, build a true expertise, even if for the purpose of living more authentically as a person and as a believer. To put it very simply, it would be much better if our catechesis, homilies, and pastoral guidance include more phrases like "it sometimes seems that . . . ," "the world seems to have trends like . . . ," "it's easy to encounter common attitudes like . . . ," and so on.

The complexity of the modern world demands on the part of pastors, educators, parents, and catechists a degree of respect and caution in assessing the reality around us. Perhaps more than ever before, these roles demand both a great love for the people one serves and a love of learning. Calmness, patience, courage, and vision are all necessary to process and assess all that goes on inside and outside the Christian community. This is true in both our personal and ministerial relationships. The Wisdom that "comes from above" (Jas 3:17) perfects and enlivens all that is genuinely human. In other words, "grace does not destroy nature, but perfects it." To academics and cultural leaders gathered at Cagliari in Italy, Francis recommended:

> It is important to interpret reality by looking it in the face. Ideological or partial interpretations are useless; they only feed illusion and disillusionment. It is important to interpret reality, but also to live this reality without fear, without fleeing, without catastrophism. . . . Discernment is neither blind nor improvised: it is carried out on the basis of ethical and spiritual criteria; it involves asking oneself about what is good, it entails thinking about our own values regarding man and the world, a vision of the person in all his dimensions, especially the spiritual and transcendent; the person may never be considered "human material"![1]

[1] Francis, Meeting with the World of Culture, September 22, 2013: https://w2.vatican.va/content/francesco/en/speeches/2013/september/documents/papa-francesco_20130922_cultura-cagliari.html.

The ideological interpretations Francis refers to here are very often the result of a tendency to *ideologize faith*. By ideology I mean a compact body of knowledge that is closed to discussion, the exclusive property of a group of enlightened ones who impose it on others and for whom it is the hallmark of their own identity, specifically because it is accepted *in toto* and without question; questions are not permitted; doubts or different emphases are not tolerated; intellectual investigation is stifled by the imposition of rigid and sterile patterns (one thinks of certain areas of philosophical and theological research). On a practical level, these assumptions result in:

- a dogmatic and overconfident approach to articulating the moral principles of bioethics, sexual ethics, and family life (deliberately ignoring other areas, especially social, political, and economic ones)

- excessive attention to the way these topics are treated in the media (especially television)

- a refusal to discuss and dialogue with those who think differently, both inside and outside the Catholic Church

- an absolute equation of fidelity to Christ with fidelity to these principles

- a complete rejection of any possibility of graduality or growth, insisting instead that everything must be accepted fully and immediately

The result is that we sometimes seem to be in a big supermarket of faith: there are no longer people, only products (as the pope says, the person becomes "human material"); a few moral principles to take from the shelves, put into one's cart, and take home, immediately and without question; speed, convenience, and quality of the product are indistinguishable. You either believe or you are considered to be the opposition. You are either in or you are out.

It should come as no surprise that Francis's gentleness and his smile are, for those who ideologize faith in such a way, a source of scandal. Nor should it be surprising when, in this context, his calls for sincerity, for the rediscovery of God's mercy, and for simple and deep discipleship arouse resentment. And it should also be no surprise that the pope would reject as inadequate any reference to "non-negotiable values." Let us recall the comment he offered in his *Corriere della Sera* interview:

> I have never understood the expression "non-negotiable values." Values are values, and that's it. I can't say among all of the fingers of the hand, one is less useful than the others. And so I don't understand how one can speak of negotiable values.[2]

Faith is not an ideology. Indeed, faith is to ideology as day is to night. Francis himself reminds us:

> Ideologues falsify the Gospel. Every ideological interpretation, from wherever it originates, on one side or the other, is a falsification of the Gospel. And these ideologues—as we have seen in the history of the Church—always end up revealed to be intellectuals with no talent, ethicists with no goodness. And let's not mention beauty, because they don't understand it. [Rather,] the way of love, the way of the Gospel is simple: it is the way the saints have followed! The saints are those who lead the church forward, [those who follow] the way of conversion, the way of humility, of love, of the heart, the way of beauty.[3]

[2] Ferruccio de Bortoli, Intervista: "Benedetto XVI non è una statua; Partecipa alla vita della Chiesa," *Corriere della Sera*, March 5, 2014: http://www.corriere.it/cronache/14_marzo_04/vi-racconto -mio-primo-anno-papa-90f8a1c4-a3eb-11e3-b352-9ec6f8a34ecc .shtml (my translation).

[3] Francis, Morning Homily in the *Domus Sanctae Marthae* Chapel, April 19, 2013: http://w2.vatican.va/content/francesco/it/cotidie

An ideological faith, moreover, tends to be easily ignored by those in political power, especially where the government supports the church with subsidies and privileges. It therefore weakens and destroys the church's prophetic witness. Not surprisingly, Francis is clear on this point:

> True prophecy is never ideological, it is not compared to the institution: it is the institution. Prophecy is institutional. True prophecy is not ideological, it is not "trendy," but is always a sign of contradiction according to the Gospel, as Jesus was. Jesus, for example, was a sign of contradiction for the religious authorities of his time: the Pharisee and Sadducee leaders, the doctors of the law. And He also was for other options and proposals: Essenes, Zealots, and so on.[4]

It is also important to understand the ideological attitude toward history. Marco Ventura makes a lucid distinction between being *faithful* and being *credulous*:

> To be faithful means to put oneself at the service of history, entering fully into it in order to explore its borders. For the faithful, history is a story of continually overcoming oneself, being at times its subject and at times its object and allowing the two roles to discover each other. The credulous, however, exploit history, standing apart from it and paying attention only to the pieces of it that they need. For the credulous, history is all about self-

---

/2013/documents/papa-francesco-cotidie_20130419_contro-ideologia .html (my translation).

[4] Francis, Address to Participants in the Italian Conference of Major Superiors (CISM), November 7, 2014: http://m.vatican.va/content /francescomobile/en/speeches/2014/november/documents/papa -francesco_20141107_conferenza-italiana-superiori-maggiori.html.

affirmation, carefully spinning the story with the aim
of controlling the present and dominating the future.[5]

Being "at the service of history" is denied by the credulous
and replaced by a fundamentalist attitude and by a strong
desire to impose oneself on the cultural and political level.
These same Catholics would have no hesitation in describ-
ing some Jews or Muslims as fundamentalists. Recall that
fundamentalism is precisely the desire to fully impose the
principles of one's ideology or religion on the political, economic, and social life. That aspiration is carried not only by
some Muslims and some Jews; there are plenty of Catholics
who seek it too. They become fundamentalists when they
decide they want to impose their beliefs on everyone, when
they stop respecting cultural and religious diversity, when
they demand that the laws of the state conform totally to
their religious beliefs (specifically those related to bioethical
issues; other beliefs often seem less important to them), when
the *truth* they believe becomes a cudgel with which to control
and subdue those who think differently, and so on. To these
people, one can apply the thinking of Romano Guardini,
who wrote, "When some people speak of truth, there is no
difference between this truth and a slap, except that they are
hitting with a word instead of with their hand."[6]

The risk of fundamentalism was identified effectively by
Pope John Paul II:

> Nor does the Church close her eyes to the danger of
> fanaticism or fundamentalism among those who, in the
> name of an ideology which purports to be scientific or

[5] Marco Ventura, *Creduli e credenti. Il declino di Stato e Chiesa come
questione di fede* (Torino: Einaudi, 2014), 21.

[6] Romano Guardini, *Briefe über Selbstbildung* (Mainz: Grünewald,
1985); translation from the Italian *Lettere sull'autoformazione* (Brescia:
Morcelliana, 1994), 21.

religious, claim the right to impose on others their own concept of what is true and good. *Christian truth* is not of this kind. Since it is not an ideology, the Christian faith does not presume to imprison changing socio-political realities in a rigid schema, and it recognizes that human life is realized in history in conditions that are diverse and imperfect. Furthermore, in constantly reaffirming the transcendent dignity of the person, the Church's method is always that of respect for freedom.[7]

The Christian faith has never been and will never be truly an ideology, much less fundamentalist in nature. For the faithful, faith is authentic encounter with a person, the Lord Jesus. Faith is a desire that compels the believer to say from her depths, "We want to see Jesus" (John 12:21). It means encountering Jesus in the many circumstances of life and hearing his loving invitation, "Follow me" (Mark 10:21).

Several times Pope Francis has linked fundamentalist attitudes to their gnostic roots, placing himself in a long line of thinkers that includes Eric Voegelin, Jacques Maritain, Henri de Lubac, Hans Urs von Balthasar, and Romano Guardini. For example, in his address to the Fifth National Convention of the Italian Church, he said:

> A second temptation to defeat is that of gnosticism. This leads to trusting in logical and clear reasoning, which nonetheless loses the tenderness of a brother's flesh. The attraction of gnosticism is that of "a purely subjective faith whose only interest is a certain experience or a set of ideas and bits of information which are meant to console and enlighten, but which ultimately keep one

---

[7] John Paul II, Encyclical letter *Centesimus Annus* (On the Hundredth Anniversary of *Rerum Novarum*), May 1, 1991, n. 46: http://w2.vatican.va/content/john-paul-ii/en/encyclicals/documents/hf_jp-ii_enc_01051991_centesimus-annus.html.

imprisoned in his or her own thoughts and feelings"
(*Evangelii Gaudium*, n. 94). Gnosticism cannot transcend.[8]

When laypeople or clergy reduce faith to ideology, the
church runs the risk of imitating other oppressive or totalitarian institutions which, built on gnostic foundations, fail to
respect human dignity and freedom, betray justice and the
common good, ignore the well-being and growth of communities, rob believers of their prophetic witness, and deny a
place for the authentic worship of God.

To measure the degree to which any institution makes a
place for authentic dialogue, one can pay attention to whether
and in what way *questions* are permitted. In his apostolic exhortation *Evangelii Gaudium*, Francis warns against a "spiritual
worldliness," one of the signs of which is the effort to "discredit
those who raise questions."[9] The prohibition of questions is
typical of all ideological environments, but it also occurs in
other settings. (Note, for example, the opposition expressed to
the pope explored in chap. 1 above.) Eric Voegelin offered one
of the most lucid analyses of this subject. The suppression of
questions is an extremely complicated psychological phenomenon. Generally those who suppress them "know very well
that the edifice they have built is destined to collapse under
the weight of the most basic questions. And yet they do not
abandon their efforts and end up becoming true villains."[10]

---

[8] Francis, Address to the Fifth National Convention of the Italian
Church, November 10, 2015: http://w2.vatican.va/content/francesco
/en/speeches/2015/november/documents/papa-francesco_20151110
_firenze-convegno-chiesa-italiana.html.

[9] Francis, Apostolic exhortation *Evangelii Gaudium* (On the Proclamation of the Gospel in Today's World), November 24, 2013, n. 97: http://
w2.vatican.va/content/francesco/en/apost_exhortations/documents
/papa-francesco_esortazione-ap_20131124_evangelii-gaudium.html.

[10] Eric Voegelin, *Wissenschaft, Politik und Gnosi* (Munchen: Kösel,
1959); translated here from the Italian edition, *Il mito del mondo nuovo*.

The ultimate motivation for this is rooted not in seeking the truth but rather in believing oneself *to be the truth*—truth that must be accepted by all, without discussion and certainly without question. In such a context, one person's thinking becomes *dogma* imposed on all, and that person inches toward the sort of atrocities that are typical of dictatorships and tyrannies, which are, according to Francis, "types of logic that have imposed and oppressed and have not sought the good of people but, on the contrary, power, success, and profit."[11]

Finally, and not least in importance, we must consider Francis's style of communicating. From the beginning of his ministry as bishop of Rome, he has demonstrated remarkable communication skills. Paradoxically, he is not comfortable with "mass communications." In the 2013 Spadaro interview, Francis commented, "I manage to look at individual persons, one at a time, to enter into personal contact with whomever I have in front of me. I'm not used to the masses."[12]

This explanation suggests the pope is familiar with the motto *Cor ad cor loquitur*, which was so dear to John Henry Newman. I do not think it is an exaggeration to apply to Francis what Jean Guitton wrote of Newman:

> *Cor ad cor loquitur*, heart speaks to heart. I find it very beautiful. It describes the eloquence, the style, the communication that people have with each other, the compassion, the eternity. It describes all of that. It reminds us

Saggi sui movimenti rivoluzionari del nostro tempo (Milano: Rusconi, 1990), 74–75.

[11] Francis, Video-Message to Participants in the Initiative Entitled "Ten Squares for Ten Commandments," June 8, 2013: https://w2.vatican.va/content/francesco/en/messages/pont-messages/2013/documents/papa-francesco_20130608_videomessaggio-10piazze.html.

[12] Antonio Spadaro, Interview with Pope Francis: https://w2.vatican.va/content/francesco/en/speeches/2013/september/documents/papa-francesco_20130921_intervista-spadaro.html.

that in any true communication, what matters is neither the words, nor the dialectic, nor the concepts. It is the interiority of one person speaking to the interiority of the other.[13]

In sum, the capacity for authentic communication begins with one person's contact with another person, even if the other is one member of a large assembly. Francis writes: "Listening, in communication, is an openness of heart which makes possible that closeness without which genuine spiritual encounter cannot occur."[14]

Simplicity does not mean superficiality or the absence of depth. The expression of profound truths in simple words is precisely the style of the Gospel. Using big, empty, and bombastic words is more typical of ideologues. Eric Voegelin described well the ways ideologues vulgarize intellectual and political debate, demonstrating themselves to be "functional illiterates with a strong desire for personal aggrandizement."[15] Francis, however, is precisely the opposite. Some say he speaks "too simply." Honestly, I have never understood whether this criticism is born of a desire to help the pope to be, like every believer, more responsive to the logic of the Gospel or simply a disguised effort to ideologize the pope and the life of the church itself.

[13] Jean Guitton, *Le Christ de ma vie. Dialogue avec Jean Dorè* (Paris: Desclee, 1987), 167.

[14] Francis, *Evangelii Gaudium*, n. 171.

[15] Eric Voegelin, *Autobiographical Reflections* (Columbia: University of Missouri Press, 2006), 77.

Chapter 5

Power within the Vatican Walls

O n March 13, 2013, when the new pope appeared at central loggia of Saint Peter's Basilica, the balcony of blessings, he referred to himself as the bishop of Rome. Among other innovations, he bowed his head and asked for "the prayer of the people asking the blessing for their bishop."[1] Since this time, with an original style, he has repeatedly raised "the power question," in the church and in the world, with a variety of words and gestures.

The issue is addressed in an interesting bit of dialogue during his 2013 interview with Eugenio Scalfari:

Scalfari: Is your Church ready and equipped to carry out this task [of love]?

Pope: What do you think?

Scalfari: I think love for temporal power is still very strong within the Vatican walls and in the institutional structure of the whole Church. I think that the institution dominates the poor, missionary Church that you would like.

---

[1] Francis, First Greeting of the Holy Father Pope Francis, March 13, 2013: http://w2.vatican.va/content/francesco/en/speeches/2013/march /documents/papa-francesco_20130313_benedizione-urbi-et-orbi.html.

Pope: In fact, that is the way it is, and in this area you
cannot perform miracles.[2]

In fact, rather than miracles, Francis has inherited a lot of
problems related to power and the management of economic
resources. These issues were recurring themes in the discussions among the cardinals prior to the Argentine pope's election. Power and money have always been major problems of
institutional life and also, partly for that reason, the object of
attention by the church's Magisterium. There are many references in the teaching of various popes. I will mention just a few.

Paul VI criticized an "exclusive search for self-interest and
power."[3] John Paul II did the same for "the all-consuming
desire for profit [and] the thirst for power" that are "indissol-
ubly united, with one or the other predominating" in today's
world.[4] Benedict XVI spoke of the "false 'gods'" of "material
possessions, possessive love, or power."[5]

Francis summarizes this thinking in *Evangelii Gaudium*:
"The thirst for power and possessions knows no limits."[6]
He adds elsewhere that often "an apostle turns his service

---

[2] Eugenio Scalfari, "The Pope: How the Church Will Change,"
La Repubblica, October 1, 2013: http://www.repubblica.it/cultura
/2013/10/01/news/pope_s_conversation_with_scalfari_english
-67643118/?refresh_ce.

[3] Paul VI, Encyclical letter *Populorum Progressio* (On the Development
of Peoples), March 26, 1967, n. 26: http://w2.vatican.va/content/paul
-vi/en/encyclicals/documents/hf_p-vi_enc_26031967_populorum
.html.

[4] John Paul II, Encyclical letter *Sollicitudo Rei Socialis* (On the Twentieth Anniversary of *Populorum Progressio*), December 30, 1987, n. 37:
http://w2.vatican.va/content/john-paul-ii/en/encyclicals/documents
/hf_jp-ii_enc_30121987_sollicitudo-rei-socialis.html.

[5] Benedict XVI, Meeting with Disadvantaged Young People of the
Rehabilitation Community of the University of Notre Dame, July 18,
2008: https://w2.vatican.va/content/benedict-xvi/en/speeches/2008
/july/documents/hf_ben-xvi_spe_20080718_darlinghurst.html.

[6] Francis, Apostolic exhortation *Evangelii Gaudium* (On the Proclamation of the Gospel in Today's World), November 24, 2013, n. 56: http://

into power, and his power into a commodity in order to gain worldly profit or even greater power,"[7] and he warns against becoming "obsessed with power"[8] and promoters of corruption, as I will discuss below.

On the ecclesial landscape, then, profit and power sometimes dominate the scene. People and plots, groups and strategies have often been linked by both elements. Among the problems related to power that were on the pontiff's table at the time of his election are careerism of priests and bishops, the administration of the Vatican Bank, the Vatican's finances and assets, lack of motivation in priestly ministry, the scandal of pedophilia, the lack of commitment to justice and the poor, the hidden forms of violence, leaks and a lack of confidentiality.

How, it is sometimes asked—almost as a joke in some sectors of both church and society—can all of this be possible among people who have pledged allegiance to such high and demanding ethical and religious principles? A passage of *Evangelii Gaudium* addresses the same question:

> It is striking that even some who clearly have solid doctrinal and spiritual convictions frequently fall into a lifestyle which leads to an attachment to financial security, or to a desire for power or human glory at all cost, rather than giving their lives to others in mission.[9]

---

w2.vatican.va/content/francesco/en/apost_exhortations/documents/papa-francesco_esortazione-ap_20131124_evangelii-gaudium.html.

[7] Francis, Presentation of Christmas Greetings to the Roman Curia, December 22, 2014: https://w2.vatican.va/content/francesco/en/speeches/2014/december/documents/papa-francesco_20141222_curia-romana.html.

[8] Francis, Meeting with the Participants in the Fifth Convention of the Italian Church, November 10, 2015: https://w2.vatican.va/content/francesco/en/speeches/2015/november/documents/papa-francesco_20151110_firenze-convegno-chiesa-italiana.html.

[9] Francis, *Evangelii Gaudium*, n. 80.

This lifestyle takes root gradually. "We don't become corrupt people overnight," Francis told journalist Andrea Tornielli; "It is a long, slippery slope that cannot be identified simply as a series of sins."[10]

Francis's analysis seems to be in line with that of Manfred Kets de Vries, who writes, "Power is a powerful narcotic—animating, life-sustaining, addictive. The people who have it generally have worked hard to obtain it and are not over-keen to let it go. This addiction poses a completely different set of power-related problems for the individual and the organization."[11]

If this is the case even in many areas of Catholic life, then Francis's reform cannot fail to include the places in which those who wield power in the church are selected and trained: seminaries, the Vatican offices that appoint and control bishops, schools of formation for the laity, diocesan curiae, and the central administration of religious orders. Power establishes its *narcotic character* very early and in a diffusive way: even small omissions or irresponsibility in training and selection leads, as though toward a large waterfall, to the sorts of degeneration addressed here.

We must include a special note on the relationship between power and violence. A few years ago, Camilo Maccise caused quite a stir with an important essay on violence in the church.[12] The author, a noted expert on ecclesial culture, began with the observation that although physical violence is no longer used or defended by today's church, other forms of violence, moral and psychological, remain with us. In a

[10] Francis, *The Name of God Is Mercy: A Conversation with Andrea Tornielli*, trans. Oonagh Stransky (New York: Random House, 2016), 82.

[11] Manfred F. R. Kets de Vries, *Leaders, Fools and Impostors: Essays on the Psychology of Leadership* (San Francisco: Jossey-Bass, 1993), 38.

[12] Camilo Maccise, "Violence in the Church," *The Tablet* (November 22, 2003): 8–9.

concise analysis, Maccise puts his finger accurately on the problems. He recognizes ecclesial settings—at the levels of the Vatican, dioceses, parishes, and religious orders—in which violence is used in various ways. Without in any way demonizing the concept of power within the church and without pointing fingers, Maccise addresses the difficult relationship between some church structures and the use of forms of violence. Among these, he notes the practice of centralization, patriarchal authoritarianism, discriminatory behaviors, and dogmatism. We should also note that he points out that the model of the church that one adopts in one's own thinking affects the way he or she conceives of and exercises power. This can result in power exercised either as violence or as a form of service that is open to discussion and dialogue in the search for truth, without dogmatism and prejudice.

Jorge Mario Bergoglio is aware of the human and educational deficits that burden the Catholic Church, especially among bishops and priests. This is clear in this long anecdote he offered:

> Once, when I had just been appointed master of novices in 1972, I took the results of a personality test to the psychologist, it was a simple test that was done as one of the elements of discernment. She was a good woman, and also a good doctor. She said to me: "This one has this problem, but he can proceed if he does so in this way. . . ." She was also a good Christian, but in some cases was adamant: "This one cannot" — "But doctor, this young man is so good" — "He is good now, but know that there are young people who unconsciously know, they are not aware of it, but unconsciously they feel that they are mentally ill, and seek strong structures that will protect them in life, in order to go on. And they go on fine, until the moment comes when they feel well established and there the problems begin" — "It seems a bit strange to me. . . ." And I will never forget her response,

it was like that of the Lord to Ezekiel: "Father, have you ever wondered why there are so many police officers who torture? They enter young, they seem healthy but when they feel confident the illness begins to emerge. Those are the strong institutions that these unconsciously sick ones seek: the police, the army, the clergy. . . . And we all know that there are many illnesses which come out." It's curious. When I realize that a young man is too rigid, too fundamentalist, I do not have confidence; in the background there is something that he himself does not know. But when they feel confident . . . Ezekiel 16, I cannot remember the verse, but it is when the Lord tells his people all that he did for them: he found them when they were just born, and he clothed them, he espoused them . . . "And then, when you felt secure, you prostituted yourself." It is a rule, a rule of life.[13]

This "prostituting" of oneself in the name of a sense of security is a constant of institutional life: maintaining strong ideals always invites the risk of some members employing mechanisms of corruption and violence to support them. When the formation of the ecclesial community and its structures of control is not attended to in a serious way; when there is no dialogue, listening to one another in the sincere search for truth and without inquisitorial attitudes; when centralization prevents leaders from having direct experience of the challenges and problems inside and outside the church—in these circumstances, the temptation to violence is always close at hand.

In such cases, it is hypocritical to try to hide the problems, and it is small-minded to use continuous justifications and pseudo-ethical reasoning to put in a better light the unhealthy

---

[13] Francis, Address to Participants in the Convention Sponsored by the Congregation for the Clergy on the Fiftieth Anniversary of the Conciliar Decrees *Optatam Totius* and *Presbyterorum Ordinis*, November 20, 2015: https://w2.vatican.va/content/francesco/en/speeches/2015/november/documents/papa-francesco_20151120_formazione-sacerdoti.html.

actions of the violent, who are often protected by a blanket of indifference or honor. Not infrequently, the choices made by those in positions of responsibility are justified as being done for the good of the institution—forgetting that the point of the institution is the good of those who make it up. And yet "the good of the institution" is invoked to justify actions that ignore or run contrary to the good of some or all of its members. We see this in politics, where "reasons of State" is sometimes the justification used to support practices that disrespect or radically deny fundamental ethical principles.

The good of the institution does not exist apart from the good of people. Institutions, to use Douglas's expression, often make life-and-death decisions.[14] In not a few cases, the common good is given cursory acknowledgment, while decisions are made that compromise or trample on the dignity and the good of individual people. The same happens in communities of religious faith, which can also be prone to ignore the common good and respect the rights of all in the name of "the good of the institution."

Pope Francis has not hesitated to shine a light on these kinds of violence, infidelity, and betrayal of the church's most basic ethical principles. In his 2014 Christmas message to the Roman Curia, he described fifteen "spiritual diseases" that afflict the church. These include:

1. thinking one is immortal, immune, or downright indispensable
2. the "Martha complex" of "excessive busy-ness"
3. mental and spiritual "petrification"
4. excessive planning and functionalism
5. poor coordination
6. spiritual Alzheimer's disease
7. rivalry and vainglory

[14] Mary Douglas, *How Institutions Think* (Syracuse: Syracuse University Press, 1986), 111–28.

8. existential schizophrenia
9. gossiping, grumbling, and back-biting
10. idolizing superiors
11. indifference to others
12. a lugubrious face
13. hoarding
14. closed circles
15. worldly profit[15]

These fifteen diseases are all related, directly or indirectly, to the exercise of power in the church and also, in many ways, in the world. Putting aside the immediacy of the language, one easily notices how well the pope's thoughts reflect academic literature on the problems of power and leadership from anthropological and ethical perspectives (see, for example, the aforementioned texts by Douglas and Kets de Vries). Francis is well aware that it is a mistake to think that issues related to the exercise of power are unrelated to ecclesial life. They are inseparable from the human condition, and for this reason, each of us is faced with ethical decisions that touch on them. In other words, every man or woman who holds power, even within the church, is first of all a *person*; he or she possesses a body, a mind, and an emotional life that exist in relationship with the self, with others, with God, and with nature.[16]

Francis is very interested in the human and relational aspects of power. In any of these fundamental relationships,

---

[15] Francis, Presentation of the Christmas Greetings to the Roman Curia, December 22, 2014: https://w2.vatican.va/content/francesco /en/speeches/2014/december/documents/papa-francesco_20141222 _curia-romana.html.

[16] Cf. Francis, Encyclical letter *Laudato Sì* (On Care for Our Common Home), May 24, 2015, nos. 66, 70, 141: http://w2.vatican.va/content /francesco/en/encyclicals/documents/papa-francesco_20150524 _enciclica-laudato-si.html.

the exercise of power calls for a special mind-set and specific ethical choices. Key points of his thinking on this, as reflected in some of his magisterial writings, must include:

1. *Power over ourselves*: Francis, a true Jesuit, makes frequent reference to the themes of interior purification, conversion, and renewal, because they keep us from falling under the power of worldly idols. They call us to make room for the power of God at work in us: "[W]e are all called to receive with an open mind and heart the Word of God which the Church imparts every day, because this Word has the capacity to change us from within. Only the Word of God has this capacity to change us from the inside, from our deepest roots. The Word of God has this power."[17]

2. *Power in relation to God*, to whom we must respond: "Before all else, the Gospel invites us to respond to the God of love who saves us, to see God in others and to go forth from ourselves to seek the good of others. Under no circumstance can this invitation be obscured! All of the virtues are at the service of this response of love."[18]

3. *Power that we exercise over others*: "We must regain the conviction that we need one another, that we have a shared responsibility for others and the world, and that being good and decent are worth it. We have had enough of immorality and the mockery of ethics, goodness, faith and honesty. It is time to acknowledge that light-hearted superficiality has done us no good."[19]

---

[17] Francis, General Audience, September 3, 2014: https://w2.vatican.va/content/francesco/en/audiences/2014/documents/papa-francesco_20140903_udienza-generale.html.

[18] Francis, *Evangelii Gaudium*, n. 39.

[19] Francis, *Laudato Sì*, n. 229.

4. *Power over nature*: The precarious state of the planet compelled the pope to say: "If we acknowledge the value and the fragility of nature and, at the same time, our God-given abilities, we can finally leave behind the modern myth of unlimited material progress. A fragile world, entrusted by God to human care, challenges us to devise intelligent ways of directing, developing and limiting our power."[20]

All these efforts by the pope to describe what the authentic exercise of power really looks like have become, for some, bothersome. Francis mentions this in *Evangelii Gaudium*, with specific reference to economic responsibility, but it would not be forcing his point unduly to apply his words to the other institutional diseases he has identified elsewhere:

> How many words prove irksome to this system! It is irksome when the question of ethics is raised, when global solidarity is invoked, when the distribution of goods is mentioned, when reference is made to protecting labour and defending the dignity of the powerless, when allusion is made to a God who demands a commitment to justice. At other times these issues are exploited by a rhetoric which cheapens them. Casual indifference in the face of such questions empties our lives and our words of all meaning.[21]

Here too, Francis's thinking is similar to what we find in anthropological and ethical studies of the nature of power; the more incisive these studies are, the more irksome they become to those who live for power and profit in so many ways.

What happens in the Christian community when attention is given to critical issues like corruption, abuse of power, and

---

[20] Ibid., n. 78.
[21] Francis, *Evangelii Gaudium*, n. 203.

the betrayal of its most fundamental purposes is the same thing that happens in all institutions at such a time. Those who have responsibilities—whether they are cardinals, bishops, priests, religious, or lay faithful—rather than being open to change, begin a process in which, according to Jung, they emphasize their strengths and push into a *shadow zone* their dark and problematic sides, the attitudes and practices that compromise authentic personhood.[22]

The "shadows" in question are classical ones, such as narcissism, perfectionism, pride, avarice, envy, anger, masochism, sadism, histrionics, arrogance, vindictiveness, unbridled ambition, demagoguery, populism, deception, vainglory, violence, aggression, sociopathy, cynicism, and hypocrisy—that is, the most deleterious aspects of the human personality. And so the strong reactions to the pope's efforts to shed light on these evils are not surprising, nor is the complete lack of interest by those in question in recognizing their own shadow zones or in renewing their faithfulness and sense of justice.

The reaction to the pope's denunciation of these evils has taken two basic forms, both of which are common in such situations: to personalize the conflict and to label the reformer.

"Personalization of conflict" is a process that aims to shift attention from the objective practices and circumstances being criticized to the subjective characteristics of the one who draws attention to them. In other words, there is an effort to ignore the moral concerns and proposals raised by the one trying to improve the institution—in this case, the pope—and to focus instead on the one who raises them, attacking him personally, in ways both valid and illegitimate. This personalization of

---

[22] See Carl Jung, *Aion*, vol. 9, bk. 2, of *Collected Works of C. G. Jung* (Princeton, NJ: Princeton University Press, 1979); and "On the Psychology of the Unconscious," in *Two Essays on Analytical Psychology*, vol. 7 of *Collected Works of C. G. Jung* (Princeton, NJ: Princeton University Press, 1972).

conflict is common in institutions that maintain degenerated and corrupt processes, organized to run parallel to authentic systems (for example, organized crime, dictatorships, and totalitarian systems). To offer an analogy, I refer to the way gangrenous tissue tends to expand on an otherwise healthy body. When someone, like the pope, points out a problem, the members of the institution have two roads before them: the first is to recognize the validity of the criticism, acknowledge its coherence with the institution's foundational principles, and undertake reform; the second is to reject every element of the criticism and to focus on the one who offers it.

Those who take the second path shift the conflict from the topic of corruption to those who are denouncing it. If the stakes are very high—*in primis*, power and money—this personalization will typically be accompanied by a second approach: the "labeling" of the one who proposes reform.

We have mentioned already the adjectives—here we can call them labels—that critics have used to describe Pope Francis: communist, pauperist, doctrinally weak, destroyer of the church, heretic, ecologist, betrayer of tradition, contrary to Catholic teaching on family, inappropriate wardrobe, exaggerated in some gestures, a Jesuit who wants to be Franciscan, too plainspoken, reckless, simplistic, undiplomatic, and so on. As happens in all institutions, these accusations have been leveled in various ways: gossip, calumny, vengeance, slander, defamation, coldness, and innuendo offered through books, newspaper articles, websites, television programs, and so on. In general, labels are used, with a sort of technical precision, to discredit those who criticize and to paint them as deluded visionaries or extremists, lovers of attention or servants of an imagined enemy. We can say of each instance what Alda Merini wrote with regard to calumny: "It is a toothless statement that, when it hits its mark, has jaws of iron."[23]

---

[23] Alda Merini, *Fiore di poesia: 1951–1997* (Torino: Einaudi, 1998), 235.

Clergy and laity who are corrupt do not take long to make use of iron jaws. The violence comes when they realize they have been caught in their corruption, and they respond by every means available. The more highly regarded one is within the socio-cultural system, the more he will tend, generally, to defend himself, denying the existence of the problems being denounced and attempting to silence those who have revealed them. In the case of the church today, the person the corrupt wish to silence is Francis. In general, these processes of institutional reform become opportunities for those who are criticized, at every level of responsibility, to demonstrate their belief in justice, peace, and the common good. Often, however, they reveal themselves to be envious and untruthful cynics and slanderers, ready to use violence (verbal or otherwise) to destroy those who criticize them and who seek to improve the institution.

Jorge Mario Bergoglio is a man who is free and secure. He understands, by experience and careful study, the tactics of personalization of conflict and labeling. As a Jesuit, he endured rejection, suspicion, and calumny. Miguel Yanez, a fellow Jesuit and close collaborator of Francis over many years, explains: "He has had a difficult life, with so many misunderstandings. Right up to the day he was elected pope, much of the Jesuit order had a negative view of Bergoglio, based, I think, on calumny."[24]

The calumnies, and more, continue, and Francis is well aware. In the face of it, the pope remains "silent. . . . He is a man of great inner conviction, he faces problems, he doesn't ignore them, but possesses an inner light, a practical wisdom, by which he always finds a way forward."[25]

---

[24] H. M. Yanez, ed., *Evangelii gaudium: il testo ci interroga. Chiavi di lettura e prospettive* (Rome: Gregorian & Biblical Press, 2015), 164.

[25] Ibid., 166.

He also has a strong dose of patience. Note his words in the Spadaro interview:

> I see the holiness . . . in the patience of the people of God: a woman who is raising children, a man who works to bring home the bread, the sick, the elderly priests who have so many wounds but have a smile on their faces because they served the Lord, the sisters who work hard and live a hidden sanctity. This is for me the common sanctity. I often associate sanctity with patience: not only patience as *hypomoné* [the New Testament Greek word], taking charge of the events and circumstances of life, but also as a constancy in going forward, day by day. This is the sanctity of the militant church also mentioned by St. Ignatius. This was the sanctity of my parents: my dad, my mom, my grandmother Rosa who loved me so much. In my breviary I have the last will of my grandmother Rosa, and I read it often. For me it is like a prayer. She is a saint who has suffered so much, also spiritually, and yet always went forward with courage.[26]

Patience, faith, tenacity, and practical wisdom all support Francis in his work of reform. All this does not mean that he is not affected by what is going on around him. It seems possible to discern several autobiographical references in the pope's comments to pilgrims about the newly beatified Oscar Romero:

> I would also like to add something that perhaps we have neglected. Monsignor Romero's martyrdom was not precise at the moment of his death; it was a martyrdom-testimony, of previous suffering, of previous

[26] Antonio Spadaro, Interview with Pope Francis: https://w2.vatican.va/content/francesco/en/speeches/2013/september/documents/papa-francesco_20130921_intervista-spadaro.html.

persecution, up to his death. But also after because, once dead—I was a young priest and I was a witness of this— he was defamed, calumniated, soiled, that is, his martyr- dom continued even by his brothers in the priesthood and the episcopate. I am not speaking from hearsay; I heard those things. In other words, it is nice to see him like this: a man who continues to be a martyr. Well now I do not think anyone dares. However, after giving his life, he continued to give it, letting himself be scourged by all those misunderstandings and calumnies.

Moving immediately from the subject of Romero, the pope adds a personal note:

That gives me strength, God only knows. [In the original Spanish of the audience text: *Eso a mí me da fuerza, solo Dios sabe.*] Only God knows the history of persons and how many times, persons who have already given their life or who have died, are continued to be scourged with the hardest stone that exists in the world: the tongue.[27]

Francis seems to be well aware that he is undergoing a "stoning" with "the hardest stone that exists in the world: the tongue." Nevertheless, he has entrusted himself to God's care, and he is moving forward: *Eso a mí me da fuerza, solo Dios sabe.*

[27] Francis, Address to Pilgrims Celebrating Blessed Oscar Romero, October 30, 2015, Zenit translation: https://zenit.org/articles/pope -s-address-to-pilgrims-celebrating-blessed-oscar-romero/.

Chapter 6

The Stench of Corruption
or the Smell of the Sheep

Today corruption in the world is on the agenda, and the corrupt attitude easily and immediately finds a nest in institutions, because an institution has so many branches here and there, so many heads and vice-heads that it is possible for corruption to nest there, and every institution can fall into this.[1]

During a 2015 visit to Naples, Francis offered a vivid description of the problem of corruption: "A corrupt thing is something dirty! If we find a dead animal that is deteriorating, that is 'corrupt,' it is repulsive and even smells bad. Corruption stinks! A corrupt society stinks!"[2] Later the same year, during a pastoral visit to Kenya, he condemned corrup-

---

[1] Francis, In-flight Press Conference from the Philippines to Rome, January 19, 2015: https://w2.vatican.va/content/francesco/en/speeches/2015/january/documents/papa-francesco_20150119_srilanka-filippine-conferenza-stampa.html.

[2] Francis, Meeting with the People and Various Social Categories of the Scampia Neighbourhood, March 21, 2015: https://w2.vatican.va/content/francesco/en/speeches/2015/march/documents/papa-francesco_20150321_napoli-pompei-popolazione-scampia.html.

tion again, this time in these words: "Corruption is something which creeps in. It's like sugar: it's sweet, we like it, it goes down easily. And then? We get sick! We come to a nasty end! With all that easy sugar we end up as diabetics, and our country becomes diabetic!"[3] And to journalist Andrea Tornielli, he commented, "Corruption leads people to lose the modesty that safeguards truth, goodness, and beauty."[4]

We should start with a definition of corruption. In the context of institutions and their socio-cultural context, corruption is an activity that provides direct or indirect benefits or services of any kind that are not earned or deserved to members of an institution or those connected with it in order to obtain or to maintain a favorable arrangement. The quantity and variety of crimes, people involved, strategies, and motivations allow us to say that very often corruption is truly a socio-cultural system and at the same time a criminal organization. Complaining about corruption often becomes a sort of national pastime, especially in countries that have quite a lot. But Francis does not stop simply at complaint.

The "system of corruption," which includes the clergy, was addressed by Jorge Mario Bergoglio, in his *Corrupción y pecado*, with these words:

> Corruption is not an act but a state, a personal and collective state, to which people get accustomed and in which they live. The values (or non-values) of corruption are integrated into a real culture, with a capacity for its own doctrine, its own language, and its own particular way of acting. It is a culture of pygmyism,

---

[3] Francis, Meeting with the Young People, November 27, 2015: https://w2.vatican.va/content/francesco/en/speeches/2015/november/documents/papa-francesco_20151127_kenya-giovani.html.

[4] Francis, *The Name of God Is Mercy: A Conversation with Andrea Tornielli*, trans. Oonagh Stransky (New York: Random House, 2016), 84.

> inasmuch as it gathers proselytes to bring them down
> to the level of admitted complicity.[5]

In this same book, written before his election as pope, Bergoglio seeks to explain what it means for a heart to become corrupt. He concludes that corruption is born at the moment that one begins to deny one's most fundamental relationships, for "corrupt people know nothing of fraternity or friendship, only complicity."[6] The heart of the corrupt person is "a heart stuck between its own self-contained self-sufficiency and the real impossibility of being enough for itself; it is a heart that has gone rotten by clinging too strongly to a treasure that has captured it.[7] All of this echoes the lesson of the Gospel: "Where your treasure is, there your heart will be" (Matt 6:21).

Elsewhere Pope Francis notes that corruption "is an evil that embeds itself into the actions of everyday life and spreads, causing great public scandal."[8] It extends, in other words, from the particular of the human heart to the universal of the global village, from micro to macro, from person to community.

In these and other texts, each time Pope Francis addresses the issue of corruption, he offers an anthropological and ethical analysis of institutional evil, either starting or concluding by anchoring it firmly in Scripture. The Gospel allows a distinction to be drawn between being a sinner and being corrupt, which Bergoglio summarized in the terse formula he encouraged his people to say to one another: "Yes, I'm

---

[5] Jorge Mario Bergoglio, "Corruption and Sin," in *The Way of Humility*, trans. Helena Scott (San Francisco: Ignatius Press, 2013), 45.

[6] Ibid., 38.

[7] Ibid., 24.

[8] Francis, Bull of Indiction of the Extraordinary Jubilee of Mercy *Misericordiae vultus*, April 11, 2015, n. 19: https://w2.vatican.va /content/francesco/en/apost_letters/documents/papa-francesco _bolla_20150411_misericordiae-vultus.html.

a sinner; but no, I'm not corrupt!"[9] To better explain such a formula, it is helpful to consider, concisely and carefully, the roots and the expressions of corruption. From the point of view of the Catholic magisterium, but without mentioning it explicitly, Francis's reference seems to be the concept of *structural sin*, which refers to the unjust elements of institutions and cultures that have become so accepted and have acquired such power that they are able to endanger the freedom and dignity of individual persons. John Paul II explained that these structures reinforce themselves, spread, and become the source of grave sin. Such structures "are rooted in personal sin, and thus always linked to the concrete acts of individuals who introduce these structures, consolidate them and make them difficult to remove. And thus they grow stronger, spread, and become the source of other sins, and so influence people's behavior."[10] They generate moral disorders that pervert the will of the people they touch. We could offer many examples of such structures of sin that are woven into both secular society and the church.

These preliminary comments bring us to the point of our analysis: corruption in the Catholic Church. It exists and, in some cases, is deeply rooted and widespread. Francis is unequivocal: "How much harm corrupt Christians, and corrupt priests do to the Church. What harm they do to the Church!"[11] He has said, "The temptation for corruption is

[9] Bergoglio, "Corruption and Sin," 11.

[10] John Paul II, Encyclical letter *Sollicitudo Rei Socialis* (On the Twentieth Anniversary of *Populorum Progressio*), December 30, 1987, n. 36: http://w2.vatican.va/content/john-paul-ii/en/encyclicals/documents/hf_jp-ii_enc_30121987_sollicitudo-rei-socialis.html.

[11] Francis, Morning Meditation in the Chapel of *Domus Sanctae Marthae*, November 11, 2013: https://w2.vatican.va/content/francesco/en/cotidie/2013/documents/papa-francesco-cotidie_20131111_sinners-yes.html.

always present in public life. Both political and religious."[12] And in Kenya, he was blunt: "There is corruption not just in politics but in every institution, even in the Vatican."[13] For Francis, corruption is an institutional problem, and since the church is an institution, it is not immune to the reality of corruption. Even in the Christian community, un-Christian lifestyles are often anchored to the potent combination of power and money. Various scandals related to the illicit acquisition of money preceded the Bergoglio pontificate, and they remain a reality. The ethical matrix is one of corruption, and the typologies are diverse.

In recent years, several ecclesiastical figures, in the service of the Vatican or in dioceses and religious orders around the world, have been involved in a variety of crimes. A quick summary would start with the Vatican bank and other financial institutions of the Vatican involved, all touched by issues related to:

- non-transparent administration, often failing to live up to the Vatican bank's formal name, "the Institute for the Works of Religion"

- a willingness to open accounts even for those who do not satisfy established criteria (i.e., they were neither religious orders or institutions nor individual members of them)

- non-compliance with European legislation on transparency and money laundering (a matter in which Francis has already intervened)

---

[12] "'We Need to Fight for a World without Poverty,'" INSP News Service, November 27, 2015: http://insp.ngo/exclusive-pope -francis-interview-for-street-papers/.

[13] Francis, Meeting with the Young People, November 27, 2015: https:// w2.vatican.va/content/francesco/en/speeches/2015/november /documents/papa-francesco_20151127_kenya-giovani.html.

- use of deposited funds for payment of bribes in some European nations

- return, by other countries, of capital of suspicious origins

- complicity and connivance of officials in obscure financial transactions

But there the church's financial administration exists well beyond the Vatican. There are dioceses, parishes, religious orders, and church-related organizations of various kinds (notably, in the field of health care) throughout the world. On various occasions and places, we have seen these institutions caught up in crimes such as fraudulent bankruptcy (e.g., the disappearance of an institution's money), embezzlement against the State (public funding spent for purposes other than those for which it was granted), violation of official secrets, disclosure of information and confidential documents of the Apostolic See (art. 116 *bis* of the Vatican's penal code), and improper, immoral, and illegal uses of ecclesiastical property. In sum, it is impossible to deny the presence of truly corrupt systems, even within some aspects of the life of the church.

In light of this negative picture, it is hard not to share the position of the pope, expressed in one of his 2014 weekday Mass homilies, as reported by *L'Osservatore Romano*:

> Corruption "is a sin that's right at the fingertips" of "that person with authority over others", whether his authority is "economic, political or ecclesiastical. We are all tempted by corruption. It's a sin at your fingertips".
>
> He continued that "someone has authority, he feels powerful, he feels like God". Corruption is thus "a daily temptation", into which "a politician, a businessman, a prelate" can fall.
>
> But "who pays for corruption?", Pope Francis asked. It is certainly not paid for by the one who "takes the bribe": in fact, that person is only the "intermediary".

> In reality, the Pope emphasized, "the poor pay for corruption!"[14]

Two other passages reveal his thinking further:

> Corruption takes away from the people. A corrupt person who makes corrupt deals or governs in a corrupt way or associates with others in order to do corrupt deals, robs the people.[15]
>
> Corruption prevents us from looking to the future with hope, because its tyrannical greed shatters the plans of the weak and tramples upon the poorest of the poor.[16]

As we see, the papal denunciation of corruption is driven not only by a fitting and well-founded desire to restore justice and legality within the church but also by the concern for the heavy burdens that are borne on the shoulders of the poor and the least ones.

The fact that the pope has had the courage to denounce this scourge does not mean that all clergy and lay Catholics are ready to do the same. The church in this time of Pope Francis remains marked by corruption both within the Roman Curia and in Catholic institutions around the world. In order to avoid corruption and to fight against it, we need hearts that are righteous and filled with a love for God. Francis is well aware of this. On the topic of spiritual worldliness in believers, he has written:

---

[14] Francis, Morning Meditation in the Chapel of the *Domus Sanctae Marthae*, June 16, 2014: https://w2.vatican.va/content/francesco/en /cotidie/2014/documents/papa-francesco-cotidie_20140616_price -corruption.html.

[15] Francis, In-flight Press Conference from the Philippines to Rome, January 19, 2015: https://w2.vatican.va/content/francesco/en /speeches/2015/january/documents/papa-francesco_20150119 _srilanka-filippine-conferenza-stampa.html.

[16] Francis, *Misericordiae Vultus*, n. 19.

> Those who have fallen into this worldliness look on from above and afar, they reject the prophecy of their brothers and sisters, they discredit those who raise questions, they constantly point out the mistakes of others and they are obsessed by appearances. Their hearts are open only to the limited horizon of their own immanence and interests, and as a consequence they neither learn from their sins nor are they genuinely open to forgiveness. This is a tremendous corruption disguised as a good. We need to avoid it by making the Church constantly go out from herself, keeping her mission focused on Jesus Christ, and her commitment to the poor.[17]

"Making the Church constantly go out from herself" is the solution that the pope proposes to root out the corruption that infects it. Therefore it is the community of believers that bears the primary responsibility. Certainly the corrupt individual should receive moral guidance and correction and also be punished legally if the law has been broken. But to eradicate the problem, the community's role is crucial. Models of reference and ways of working must be changed. Obviously spiritual and pastoral solutions do not exclude legal and judicial ones as well, and Francis is clearly committed to all of these. Suffice it to mention, for example, the actions of the Vatican court in punishing some of the guilty and the cooperation of the Vatican bank in some judicial investigations underway in Italy. Each of these examples reflects the thinking expressed in Francis's bull of indiction for the special Jubilee Year:

> If we want to drive [corruption] out from personal and social life, we need prudence, vigilance, loyalty, transparency, together with the courage to denounce any wrongdoing. If it is not combated openly, sooner or later everyone will become an accomplice to it, and it will end up destroying our very existence.[18]

---

[17] Francis, *Evangelii Gaudium*, n. 97.
[18] Francis, *Misericordiae Vultus*, n. 19.

Francis's stance toward internal corruption is based, however, on a hope rooted in faith, which he expresses in this way: "The Lord, however, does not tire of knocking at the doors of the corrupt. Corruption is no match for hope."[19]

On this hope rests a commitment to reform the church. The remedy for corruption, then, goes beyond the narrow scope of personal conversion and becomes communal. By adopting this stance, Francis explicitly disavows that of his opponents, which tends to minimize corruption and to relegate it strictly to the private sphere. When entrenched systems of corruption are recognized—within the church or in any other institution—there will always be those who will react superficially or by minimizing the issue.

But corruption is stronger than those who deny it, and it will continue to stink, to do real damage to the church and society, especially to the poor. Francis has undertaken a reform of the church that, in the wake of Vatican II, calls all believers to be credible signs of salvation and God's mercy for women and men today. He calls us to be, in his words, a church that is free of the stench of corruption and bears the "smell of the sheep."[20] Indeed, he asks everyone to "always take care to encounter the other, to get the 'odor' of the men of today, until you are permeated with their joys and hopes, with their sadness and anguishes."[21]

---

[19] Francis, Address to the Delegates of the International Association of Penal Law, October 23, 2014: https://w2.vatican.va/content/francesco /en/speeches/2014/october/documents/papa-francesco_20141023 _associazione-internazionale-diritto-penale.html.

[20] Francis, *Evangelii Gaudium*, n. 24.

[21] Francis, Message to the Italian Catholic University Federation (FUCI), October 14, 2014: https://zenit.org/articles/pope-s-address -to-university-students-federation/.

Chapter 7

The Weight of Scandal and the Patience of Reform

P ope Francis has repeatedly called the Christian community to authentic Christian living and, where it is lacking, to conversion, to welcoming the mercy of God, and to a renewed faithfulness to Christ. Francis has exhibited no fear of facing the wounds and scandals of the church at both the local and universal levels, and of offering reproaches, along with exhortations to repentance, where necessary. One thinks of the problems outlined in the previous chapters. All point to scandals, of small or large dimensions. But are they inevitable? Does Pope Francis bear any responsibility in their powerful emergence in recent years?

Ethics teaches us that the responsibility for a scandal rests not on the one who exposes it, with an eye to healing it, but on its instigator. Francis seems to make reference to this when he says: "The Lord Jesus once said to his disciples—it is in the Gospel: 'It is inevitable that there will be scandals. . . .' We are human beings, all of us are sinners. And there will be scandals, there will be. The issue is to prevent more from happening! In the administration of finances, honesty and transparency [are essential]."[1]

---

[1] Francis, Interview with Journalists during the Return Flight from the Holy Land, May 26, 2014: https://w2.vatican.va/content

The abuse of minors is one significant example of the important relationship between scandals and ecclesial reform. Frances addressed this question bluntly during an in-flight press conference during his return from a pastoral visit to Mexico. To a journalist's question about whether he considered meeting with victims, and his thoughts on the practice of simply moving abusive priests from one parish to another, Francis responded with a historical overview of the matter:

> Very well, I will begin with the second. A bishop who moves a priest, who has been proven to be a pedophile, to a new parish is reckless, and the best thing he can do is present his resignation. Is that clear?
>
> Second, going back to Maciel's case. And here allow me to honour a man who fought even when he did not have the power to step in, yet he did: Ratzinger. Cardinal Ratzinger deserves applause. Yes, a round of applause for him. He had all the documentation. When he was prefect of the Congregation for the Doctrine of the Faith, he took everything in his hands, he conducted investigations and he pushed forward, forward, forward . . . but he couldn't go any further in the execution. If you remember, 10 days before John Paul II died, Ratzinger told the whole Church, at the *Via Crucis* on Good Friday, that she needed to be purified of "filth". And at the *Missa pro eligendo Pontifice*—he is no fool, he knew he was going to be a candidate—he didn't care to hide his position, he said exactly the same thing. What I mean to say is that he was a brave man who helped so many open this door. Thus, I want to remind you of him, because sometimes we forget all this hidden work that laid the foundation for "taking the lid off the pot".
>
> Third, we are doing quite a lot of work. Speaking with the Cardinal Secretary of State, also with the group

---

/francesco/en/speeches/2014/may/documents/papa-francesco_20140526_terra-santa-conferenza-stampa.html.

of nine Cardinal advisors, after listening to them, I chose to appoint a third adjunct secretary to the Congregation for the Doctrine of the Faith, who is concerned solely with these cases, because the Congregation cannot manage with everything it has to do, and therefore one who knows how to deal with this. Furthermore, the Court of Appeals was established, presided by Archbishop Scicluna, which deals with cases of second instance, when there is recourse; cases of the first instance are handled by the *"feria quarta"* [the fourth day]—as we call it, because it convenes on Wednesdays—of the Congregation for the Doctrine of the Faith. When there is recourse, the case goes back to the first instance, and that is not fair. Thus, the second recourse, already having a legal profile, a defense attorney. However it needs to be evaluated—because we are rather behind in handling cases—so that cases can be presented. Another reality that is functioning very well is the Commission for the Protection of Minors. It is not strictly reserved to cases of pedophilia, but to the protection of minors. In that context I met for an entire morning with six of them—two German, two Irish and two English people—men and women, victims of abuse. And I also met with victims in Philadelphia. There too, I spent one morning meeting with victims. In other words, work is being done. But I thank God that the lid is off of this pot, and we must continue to keep it uncovered, and be attentive.

Lastly, I would like to say that this is a monstrosity. A priest is consecrated so as to lead a child to God; were he to "devour" that child in a diabolical sacrifice, he would destroy the child.[2]

---

[2] Francis, In-Flight Press Conference from Mexico to Rome, February 17, 2016: https://w2.vatican.va/content/francesco/en/speeches/2016 /february/documents/papa-francesco_20160217_messico-conferenza -stampa.html.

Francis makes reference here to the history and development of the church's response to pedophilia. Included in that history are the following significant steps.

> 2001: John Paul II, in response to growing allegations of sexual abuse of minors by clerics, signs the *motu proprio Sacramentorum Sanctitatis Tutela* (*SST*), promulgating *Norms Concerning the More Grave Delicts Reserved to the Congregation for the Doctrine of the Faith.*

> 2002: John Paul II speaks about the scandal in Boston, leads several meetings in Rome with American bishops on the issue of sexual abuse, and speaks to the American cardinals.

> 2004: John Paul II speaks to American bishops during their *ad limina* visits.

> 2005: Benedict XVI establishes a de facto "zero-tolerance policy" for the universal church, following the one already established at the national level by the United States Conference of Catholic Bishops.

> 2006: Benedict XVI addresses the issue with Irish bishops during their *ad limina* visits.

> 2008: Benedict XVI offers several speeches and interviews on the topic and meets with abuse victims in Sydney and Washington, DC.

> 2010: Benedict XVI approves the revision of John Paul II's *motu proprio SST* and adopts new norms; publishes a pastoral letter to the Catholics of Ireland on the topic of the sexual abuse of children; as the scandals widen (not only in English-speaking countries, but also in Germany, Austria, Belgium, Italy, and elsewhere), meets with victims of sexual abuse by priests in Rabat, London, and Malta; offers several speeches on the topic to bishops, young people, and the sick during a pastoral visit to the United Kingdom.

2011: The Congregation for the Doctrine of the Faith issues *Circular Letter to Assist Episcopal Conferences in Developing Guidelines for Dealing with Cases of Sexual Abuse of Minors Perpetrated by Clerics*; Benedict XVI meets with victims of sexual abuse by priests in Erfurt.

2012: Benedict XVI laicizes several hundred clerics and forces others to live and work in situations without access to minors.

2013: Francis issues the *motu proprio On the Jurisdiction of Judicial Authorities of Vatican City State in Criminal Matters*; inserts into the Vatican penal system rules regarding crimes related to child pornography and child abuse that are among the strictest in Europe.

2014: Francis compares sexual abuse to black masses and reiterates the "zero-tolerance" policy; laicizes Vatican nuncio Archbishop Jozef Wesolowski, accused of child abuse and possession of child pornography; establishes the Pontifical Commission for the Protection of Minors (headed by the American Cardinal Sean Patrick O'Malley); meets in his residence with victims of sexual abuse.

2015: Pontifical Commission for the Protection of Minors requests revision of the Vatican penal system to include punishment of bishops who cover up sexual abuse offenders; Francis meets victims of sexual abuse in the United States.

2016: Francis publishes the *motu proprio Come una Madre Amorevole,* establishing new norms providing for the removal of bishops who have been negligent with regard to sexual abuse of children.

The recent popes have addressed clergy sexual abuse through the Vatican legal system, pastoral interventions aimed at pushing the bishops to work for justice and reform at the local level, and personal meetings with victims and their families. Here the decisive point seems to be, rather than the lack of disciplinary actions, the failure by bishops to implement papal directives at the local level and, therefore, the responsibility of individual bishops in monitoring and promoting justice and renewal in the particular churches. Obviously, we remain very close to these events; it will be mainly for future historians to assess the commitment of bishops, clergy, and laypeople to applying papal guidelines and initiating and implementing the much-desired ecclesial reform, in this area as in others. In his comments cited above, Pope Francis refers to the work of Joseph Ratzinger, insisting that, first as prefect cardinal and then as pope, "he couldn't go any further in the execution." While assumptions about facts and people involved can be arbitrary, from the perspective of institutional analysis, the very phrase highlights the difficulties involved in carrying out these efforts, perhaps as much at the local level as at the global. But this too will be for historians to say.

Equally important, from the institutional point of view, is the fact that—in the pope's words—"the lid is off of this pot." Not everything can and must be known. Consequently, external critics will only be aware of some aspects of the issue. There is an eternal tension between those in power and their critics; the dialectical relationship between leaders and intellectuals is necessary and indispensable to the extent that both responsibly recognize their limitations and work together for the good of individuals and the entire community.

The pedophilia scandal is only one example of how every institutional reform project can be understood as a fight against scandal within an institution (its "shadow zones") and a commitment to correct wrongdoing. When a scandal is revealed, does everyone understand and have tools necessary to assess what is going on? Certainly not. It is no coincidence that Francis, on the occasion of a new scandal emerging at the Vatican, felt the need to point out:

I know that many of you have been troubled by the news circulating in recent days concerning the Holy See's confidential documents that were taken and published.

For this reason I want to tell you, first of all, that stealing those documents is a crime. It's a deplorable act that is of no help. I personally had asked for that study to be carried out and both my advisors and I were well acquainted with those documents, and steps have been taken that have begun to bear fruits, some of them even visible.

Therefore I wish to reassure you that this sad event certainly does not deter me from the reform project that we are carrying out, together with my advisors and with the support of all of you. Yes, with the support of the whole Church because the Church is renewed with prayer and the daily holiness of each baptized person.[3]

Scandals are inevitable, those who are responsible are punished, and the reform goes ahead, with the support of many. The pope specifies: "together with my advisors and with the support of all of you." Here we touch on another key point of every reform project. No leader—the pope included—possesses all of the skills and competencies necessary; this would be humanly impossible. Mariano Magrassi, once the archbishop of the Archdiocese of Bari, which is my home, often said that no bishop has "all the gifts," but he has "the gifts of all."[4] He is like the conductor of an orchestra who can't play all of the instruments but knows how to coordinate, harmonize, and help all of the musicians who can.

[3] Francis, Angelus, November 8, 2015: https://w2.vatican.va/content /francesco/en/angelus/2015/documents/papa-francesco_angelus _20151108.html.

[4] Mariano Magrassi, *Vivere la Chiesa*, vol. 1 (Noci: Edizioni La Scala, 1988), 215.

A reform project can proceed effectively only if the various collaborators cooperate and carry out their roles according to their abilities, professionally and ethically. They have a duty not only to work with honesty and competence but also to help the leader govern better. If this doesn't happen, the group of collaborators amounts to little more than a sort of royal court.

The literature shows that it is typical of institutions in crisis or burdened by corruption to develop such courts, powerful little groups around the leader. It can sometimes even happen that a leader may try with all his might to reform an institution, while at the same time a powerful group, a court, defends the *status quo.*

Collaborators like this are also usually involved in coordinating all kinds of slander, exclusion, deceit, deception, undermining of authentic collaborators, and the identification and sacrifice of scapegoats. The more they have to gain in privileges and profits by maintaining the status quo, the more these people are ready to carry out their ignoble work. In fact, one law of the conservation of corrupt power—Shakespeare teaches us in *Henry IV*—is that the leader leaves the dirty work to subordinates while officially knowing nothing about it.[5]

No institutional reform is without opponents. The more incisive the reform, the more detractors emerge. This goes without saying, and few will question it. The question, however, is this: how do we ensure that Pope Francis's reform becomes irreversible, even after Francis himself has passed from the scene?

From an anthropological point of view, Mary Douglas has explained that in any institution, the entrenching of an idea is a social, economic, and political process.[6] This means that

---

[5] See William Shakespeare, *Henry IV*, Part 2, Act 4, Scene 4: http://shakespeare.mit.edu/2henryiv/2henryiv.4.4.html.

[6] Mary Douglas, *How Institutions Think* (Syracuse: Syracuse University Press, 1986), 45.

there are many parties involved and many variables to be considered. Study, discernment, authentication, and, in the case of the church, a spirit of genuine faith are all essential. Cardinals, bishops, priests, professors, catechists, communications professionals, and the lay faithful all have the duty— each according to his or her own role and competence—of articulating and participating in the reform of this pope. For example, about three hundred theologians from throughout Latin America and beyond, meeting for a Continental Congress of Theology titled "The Church That Walks with the Spirit and with the Poor" (October 2015, in Belo Horizonte, Brazil), expressed solidarity with the pope and confirmed their commitment to cooperate in his reform.[7]

This intervention of the South American theologians illustrates the responsibilities of those who share and support the pope's reform. From the ethical point of view, the function of one who acts as leader is sustained only because it promotes the authentic good of all. Otherwise, we have a duty, in good conscience, not only to withdraw support but to oppose the leader by lawful means and, in some cases, perhaps means that are not. Using an analogy, we might say that in the human body, the parts support the activities of the head, because it provides for the harmonization of the good of the individual part with the good of the whole organism; if the head begins to fail in its fundamental duties, the support must be withdrawn, and measures must be taken to overcome the crisis.

It should also be remembered that no power can support itself; it arises in relation to others and for the sake of others. As soon as the one in power becomes isolated, that power easily degenerates into corruption, despotism, violence, and so on. Genuine support for the leader is expressed in various ways that are good for both the leader and for all members of

---

[7] See *Carta de apoio ao Papa Francisco* (2015) at http://www.ihu .unisinos.br/noticias/548776-carta-de-apoio-ao-papa-francisco.

the institution. Among these are study, respectfulness, trust, participation, and vigilance. This is not the place to dwell on any of them. It is useful, however, to recall a fundamental ethical principle: in every reform process, those who make up an institution must choose a position. Those who reject the efforts of the various opposition factors ought to therefore offer their support to the reform, in whatever ways they are able. There can be no limbo where one can choose to "wait it out" until the moment has passed. To do nothing is also to choose; that is, it is to choose not to cooperate with the reform. In the case of Francis's efforts, what is at stake is not simply the question of whether to follow a particular leader but whether to implement the Second Vatican Council.

On several occasions, Francis has made reference to the strategic elements of implementing reform. Particularly illuminating is this passage from the Spadaro interview:

> According to St. Ignatius, great principles must be embodied in the circumstances of place, time and people. In his own way, John XXIII adopted this attitude with regard to the government of the church, when he repeated the motto, "See everything; turn a blind eye to much; correct a little." John XXIII saw all things, the maximum dimension, but he chose to correct a few, the minimum dimension. You can have large projects and implement them by means of a few of the smallest things. Or you can use weak means that are more effective than strong ones, as Paul also said in his First Letter to the Corinthians.[8]

This sheds light on the supporting elements of Francis's reform. In my opinion, these elements are stated clearly in

---

[8] Antonio Spadaro, Interview with Pope Francis: https://w2.vatican
.va/content/francesco/en/speeches/2013/september/documents
/papa-francesco_20130921_intervista-spadaro.html.

Evangelii Gaudium, which seems to be the pastoral program of this pontificate. Indeed, Pope Francis has gone so far as to ask the church in Italy directly: "For the coming years: in every community, in every parish and institution, in every diocese and circumscription, in every region, try to launch, in a synodal fashion, a deep reflection on the *Evangelii Gaudium*, to draw from it practical parameters and to launch its dispositions."[9]

Key to understanding this document are the four principles Francis identifies in sections 221–37:

1. Time is greater than space
2. Unity prevails over conflict
3. Realities are more important than ideas
4. The whole is greater than the part

This is not the place to go into detail about each of these principles, but in our analysis of the institutional reform, it is important to note that Francis insists that "progress in building a people in peace, justice and fraternity depends on" them.[10] They take us to the heart of the Bergoglio project.

Francis's reform demands time, patience, and perseverance. He noted himself, just months after his election as pope:

> This discernment takes time. For example, many think that changes and reforms can take place in a short time. I believe that we always need time to lay the foundations for real, effective change. And this is the time of discernment. Sometimes discernment instead urges us to do precisely what you had at first thought you would

[9] Francis, Meeting with the Participants in the Fifth Convention of the Italian Church, November 10, 2015: http://w2.vatican.va/content/francesco/en/speeches/2015/november/documents/papa-francesco_20151110_firenze-convegno-chiesa-italiana.html.

[10] Francis, *Evangelii Gaudium*, n. 221.

do later. And that is what has happened to me in recent months.[11]

In *Evangelii Guadium*, he writes:

> One of the faults which we occasionally observe in so-
> ciopolitical activity is that spaces and power are pre-
> ferred to time and processes. Giving priority to space
> means madly attempting to keep everything together in
> the present, trying to possess all the spaces of power and
> of self-assertion; it is to crystallize processes and pre-
> sume to hold them back. Giving priority to time means
> being concerned about initiating processes rather than
> possessing spaces. Time governs spaces, illumines them
> and makes them links in a constantly expanding chain,
> with no possibility of return. What we need, then, is to
> give priority to actions which generate new processes
> in society and engage other persons and groups who
> can develop them to the point where they bear fruit in
> significant historical events. Without anxiety, but with
> clear convictions and tenacity.[12]

He was even clearer on this subject in his 2015 Christmas greetings to the Roman Curia. I summarize here the key
points of that address:[13]

- "The reform will move forward with determination,
  clarity and firm resolve, since *Ecclesia semper reformanda*."

- The "diseases" that afflict the Curia call for "prevention,
  vigilance, care and, sadly, in some cases, painful and
  prolonged interventions," without denying that they are

[11] Spadaro, "Interview."

[12] Francis, *Evangelii Guadium*, n. 223.

[13] Francis, Presentation of the Christmas Greetings to the Roman
Curia, December 21, 2015: https://w2.vatican.va/content/francesco
/en/speeches/2015/december/documents/papa-francesco_20151221
_curia-romana.html.

"causing no small pain to the entire body and harming many souls, even by scandal."

- "Nonetheless, diseases and even scandals cannot obscure the efficiency of the services rendered" by the Curia; for these the pope expresses "heartfelt gratitude and needed encouragement to all those good and honest men and women in the Curia who work with dedication, devotion, fidelity and professionalism, offering to the Church and the Successor of Peter the assurance of their solidarity and obedience, as well as their constant prayers."

- On the positive side, the pope offers a non-exhaustive "catalogue of needed virtues for those who serve in the Curia and for those who would like to make their consecration or service to the Church more fruitful."

- He says the following virtues are indispensable for those who wish to serve the church (noting, "It is a list based on an acrostic analysis of the word *Misericordia*— Father Ricci did this in China—with the aim of having it serve as our guide and beacon"):

1. **M**issionary and pastoral spirit
2. **I**doneity (or suitability) and sagacity
3. **S**pirituality and humanity
4. **E**xample and fidelity
5. **R**easonableness and gentleness
6. **I**nnocuousness and determination
7. **C**harity and truth
8. **O**penness and maturity
9. **R**espectfulness and humility
10. **D**iligence and attentiveness
11. **I**ntrepidness and alertness
12. **A**ccountability and sobriety

Again in this speech, Francis demonstrates the ability to weave together anthropological, ethical, and ecclesiological ideas. He not only adopts the thinking reflected in Peguy's famous aphorism—"the revolution will be moral or there will be no revolution"—but he also seeks to open a discussion about the formation and the service of those who have responsibility in the Christian community. The pope even invites the members of the Curia "to add to [the list] and to complete it."

Some critics have emphasized the harshness with which the pope has at times addressed members of the clergy and the episcopate. The fact is undeniable. An institutional analysis cannot fall into the trap of dwelling on the character of the leader, insofar as it does play a role, nor, at the same time, can the reception and implementation of the reform be dependent on the emotional state of the one who speaks or the one who listens, especially if it is a priest or a bishop. If that were the case, we would fall into a personalization of the conflict, which we have already discussed (see chap. 6). The problem—I believe—must be articulated in different terms. The leader of an institution, especially while implementing a reform, has the duty to reproach its members when appropriate and to call them to greater authenticity, provided that this is done under specific ethical conditions. These must include:

1. clarity in identifying the problems, their causes, and their frequency

2. reference to the ethical foundations of the institution

3. the identification of a plan for reform and the implementation of structural and management changes

4. forms of punishment and dismissal for those who have demonstrated attitudes contrary to the ethical foundations

5. in carrying out all of the above, especially in the church, attentiveness to both mercy and justice, so far as is humanly possible

But there is one last point to consider. Institutions are very often considered to have both affective and protective qualities, or, as some might say, both maternal and paternal. There is an extensive literature on this subject. We can summarize it by noting that we often expect leaders to possess opposing capabilities and qualities. "To command," writes Emmanuel Mounier, "is a higher form of behavior, like obedience." The French philosopher explains that it consists in anticipating, reflecting, taking action at the moment and in the way necessary, attending to forces of opposition, at times exerting and at times bending one's will, being constantly vigilant of the implementation of the order given and ensuring the necessary orientation, containing problems and correcting mistakes.[14]

But it would be both impossible and silly to try to establish standards according to which every leader is measured, according to specific levels of strictness and affection, generosity and prudence, justice and mercy, firmness in decisions and willingness to reconsider decisions, etc. It would be like constructing a theoretically ideal model of a leader and then trying to apply that model indiscriminately to all. Every leader brings to the role a particular set of characteristics, strengths, and weaknesses. These include human qualities (physical, intellectual, and emotional), an ethical make-up, and a set of acquired skills. The leader also brings a certain set of resources, material and otherwise, and, in particular, a particular group of collaborators. All this applies just as truly to the pope.

---

[14] Emmanuel Mounier, *The Character of Man*, trans. Cynthia Rowland (New York: Harper & Brothers, 1956), 184. (The initial sentence quoted here from Mounier is found in the English edition, but the rest of Mounier's thought here is omitted from the English, which is an abridged edition of the original, *Traité du caractère* [Paris: Seuil, 1947].—Trans.)

Chapter 8

The Reform
and the Perspective from Below

Will Pope Francis pull it off? The Italian intellectual Raniero La Valle offers this response:

> The answer to the question—Will he do it?—will become clear in the not too distant future. But we can begin to offer an answer today. And the answer is that the pope has, in a certain way, already done it, because there are things that, once done, cannot be undone. There are some hidden treasures that, once they are found, cannot be lost again. Once the taboo is broken, evil acts, but also good ones, can always be repeated. Francis has broken more than one taboo, and after that, things cannot be the same again.[1]

It is a difficult question, whether to take the view, like La Valle, that Francis's work is in many ways already accomplished or that the reform process is still in its early stages. The guiding principle of this institutional analysis has been

---

[1] Raniero La Valle, *Chi sono io Francesco? Cronache di cose mai viste* (Firenze: Ponte delle Grazie, 2015), 191.

anchored in the knowledge that institutions resist innovation, as an ample scientific literature demonstrates and explores. Primary among them all, Mary Douglas has lucidly noted, "Institutions share the pathetic megalomania of the computer, whose vision of the world is its own program."[2]

To put it more simply: those who are responsible for the institutional machinery can fall into the trap of thinking that their program is the best and the only one in the world and that, therefore, the institutional machine has value and power only if its program never changes and, furthermore, if it manages to impose its program always and everywhere. Francis has disrupted this scheme or, as La Valle says, broken a taboo.

Obviously, this is only the institutional aspect of the story, the subject of this book. For an analysis of the historical, theological, and spiritual aspects, I refer the reader to Anna Carfora and Sergio Tanzarella's fine book, which offers an analysis of Francis's reform in light of the prophetic voices of the church's history, especially Antonio Rosmini, Antonio Fogazzaro, Lorenzo Milani , Oscar Romero, Tonino Bello, and Raffaele Nogaro.[3]

The challenge, now as in other times and places for the Christian community, is to introduce, or to confirm where it is already present, a new perspective in the ecclesial practice: the *perspective from below*. In his letters from prison, Dietrich Bonhoeffer wrote:

> There remains an experience of incomparable value. We have for once learnt to see the great events of world history from below, from the perspective of the outcast, the suspects, the maltreated, the powerless, the oppressed, the reviled—in short, from the perspective of those who

[2] Mary Douglas, *How Institutions Think* (Syracuse: Syracuse University Press, 1986), 92.

[3] Anna Carfora and Sergio Tanzarella, *Il cristiano tra potere e mondanità. 15 gravi malattie secondo papa Francesco* (Trapani: Il Pozzo di Giacobbe, 2015), 30–81.

suffer. The important thing is that neither bitterness nor envy should have gnawed at the heart during this time, that we should have come to look with new eyes at matters great and small, sorrow and joy, strength and weakness, that our perception of generosity, humanity, justice and mercy should have become clearer, freer, less corruptible. We have to learn that personal suffering is a more effective key, a more rewarding principle for exploring the world in thought and action than personal good fortune. This perspective from below must not become the partisan possession of those who are eternally dissatisfied; rather, we must do justice to life in all its dimensions from a higher satisfaction whose foundation is beyond any talk of "from below" or "from above."[4]

Much of Francis's thinking can be interpreted through these words from Bonhoeffer. The pope's activities, comments, and teaching are all marked by a *perspective from below*. This perspective is the heart of Francis's reform: one either understands this or does not understand the reform. One either shares the perspective, thoughtfully and with a careful urgency, or one opposes the reform and dismisses it as the pope's vanity.

But let us explore a little further the meaning of Jorge Mario Bergoglio's perspective from below. The biographies attest to an indisputable fact: love for the poor, with understanding, passion, and commitment, have been a part of who he is from the start. This is reflected in the comment offered to him at the moment of his election, by his friend and colleague Cardinal Claudio Hummes: "Do not forget the poor!" Recounting the moment, the pope has explained, "And that word entered right here: the poor, the poor."[5]

---

[4] Dietrich Bonhoeffer, *Letters and Papers from Prison*, ed. Eberhard Bethke (New York: Touchstone, 1997), 17.

[5] Francis, Address to Journalists, March 16, 2013. (My translation, because by being a bit more literal than the English translation made avail-

The word may have entered his heart at that moment, but it was already there too. Now it must enter the life and ministry of the church.

> The Church must speak the truth and also with a testimony: the testimony of poverty. The believer who speaks of poverty or of the homeless, but who lives a life of luxury: that will not do. This is the first temptation.[6]

Francis's perspective from below clashes with the realities of the Catholic communities in many European and North American nations, which possess ample material goods and financial resources, enjoy various kinds of privileges from the state, and have the benefit of valuable property of all kinds. Too often, this leads the Catholic community to imbibe the values of other institutions for which the only or the primary aim is profit. Many prophetic voices have called the church to make a more deliberate choice for poverty and Christian authenticity. In Italy, we remember, above all, Fr. Primo Mazzolari, who wrote: "If people saw us earn our bread like they do, or a little more honestly than they do, religion would be welcomed with very little help from preaching or organizations. A healthy poverty is like a sip of wine: it takes away thirst but does not intoxicate."[7]

We have dioceses, parishes, religious orders, and church organizations that are too often "drunk" on the idea of profit at all costs, living a thousand miles away from authentic

---

able by the Vatican, it makes the author's point here clearer. Original here: https://w2.vatican.va/content/francesco/it/speeches/2013/march/documents/papa-francesco_20130316_rappresentanti-media.html. Published English translation here: https://zenit.org/articles/pope-francis-address-to-journalists/.—Trans.)

[6] "'We Need to Fight for a World without Poverty,'" INSP News Service, November 27, 2015: http://insp.ngo/exclusive-pope-francis-interview-for-street-papers/.

[7] Primo Mazzolari, *La pieve sull'argine* (Bologna: EDB, 1978), 260.

poverty. I offer one example among many possible, but one of strategic importance. Often within the structures of the Vatican, dioceses, and religious orders, we find financial officers, responsible for administering crucial financial and real estate holdings on behalf of popes and bishops; the ways they carry out their work, in attitudes and ethical principles, are identical to their counterparts in the political and financial worlds. But the way this work is carried out is important not only in internally, in terms of good governance and transparency; it also has the potential to bear poignant witness to the secular world.

The call of Vatican II, now more than a half century old, has fallen on deaf ears:

> The church utilizes temporal realities as often as its mission requires it. But it does not pin its hopes on privileges accorded to it by civil authority; indeed, it will give up the exercise of certain legitimate rights whenever it becomes clear that their use will compromise the sincerity of its witness, or whenever new circumstances call for a different approach.[8]

These words are so clear, they leave no room for misunderstanding. Any privilege available to the church must be evaluated in light of the evangelical witness that it offers. It will come as a surprise to some that the council calls for the church to *reject even legitimate benefits*, if they have the potential of creating doubts about the work of the church. The proclamation and living out of the Gospel should take priority over every other consideration. But is this not the lesson Francis is offering us? And isn't it the same lesson offered by Paul VI, John Paul II, and Benedict XVI?

---

[8] *Gaudium et Spes* 76, in *Vatican Council II: Constitutions, Decrees, Declarations*, ed. Austin Flannery (Collegeville, MN: Liturgical Press, 2014).

To recover the perspective from below, it is imperative that the church asks itself to what extent the logic of the market, of profit at any cost, guides our institutions and our ways of operating. These ways are not always inspired by Gospel criteria of the common good, justice, peace, and the protection of human persons. They have not always resulted in prophetic relationships with political power, perhaps out of concern for protecting preferential treatment, favorable arrangements, and economic privileges. With regard to money (internal resources, public funding, financial support for church activities and church property) there has not been adequate attention to prudent discernment.

The perspective from below also challenges in terms of sign-value. We might consider, for example, how many dioceses, parishes, and Catholic institutions have responded, and in what ways, to the pope's call, in September 2015, for the welcoming of migrants:

> As the Jubilee of Mercy approaches, I make an appeal to parishes, religious communities, monasteries and shrines throughout Europe, that they express the Gospel in a concrete way and host a refugee family. A concrete gesture in preparation for the Holy Year of Mercy. May every parish, every religious community, every monastery, every shrine of Europe welcome one family, beginning with my Diocese of Rome.[9]

Certainly some institutions have taken up the pope's request, but doubts and denials have been the more common response.

The perspective from below guides and sustains Pope Francis's reform. It sometimes seems like a big dream. But

[9] Francis, Angelus, September 6, 2015: https://w2.vatican.va/content /francesco/en/angelus/2015/documents/papa-francesco_angelus _20150906.html.

it is a useful dream, inspiring real and necessary action. In this way, it is much like the dream of Hélder Câmara, which he wrote about in one of his nightly meditations during the Second Vatican Council: "Forgive my dreams. I have such a purity of intentions, so much love for the Church, such a great dream to see her at the forefront in the fight for the humble and the poor!"[10]

Will Pope Francis pull it off? *Solo Dios sabe.*

[10] Hélder Câmara, *Correspondencia conciliar 1962–1965,* Obras Completas 1 (Recife, 2004); this translation from the Italian edition, *Roma, due del mattino. Lettere dal Concilio Vaticano II* (Cinisello Balsamo: Edizioni San Paolo, 2008), 50.

Bibliography

"Añoro ir a una pizzería y comerme una buena pizza." *La Voz del Pueblo*. May 31, 2015. http://www.lavozdelpueblo.com.ar/nota-27095--aoro-ir-a-una-pizzera-y-comerme-una-buena-pizza.

Aristotle. *Politics*. http://www.perseus.tufts.edu/hopper/text?doc=Perseus%3atext%3a1999.01.0058.

Augustine. Sermon 213. In *Sermons*. Translated by Edmund Hill. The Works of Saint Augustine III/6. New Rochelle, NY: New City Press, 1993.

Benedict XVI. Meeting with Disadvantaged Young People of the Rehabilitation Community of the University of Notre Dame. July 18, 2008. https://w2.vatican.va/content/benedict-xvi/en/speeches/2008/july/documents/hf_ben-xvi_spe_20080718_darlinghurst.html.

Bergoglio, Jorge Mario. "Corruption and Sin." In *The Way of Humility*, translated by Helena Scott. San Francisco: Ignatius Press, 2013.

Bonhoeffer, Dietrich. *Letters and Papers from Prison*. Edited by Eberhard Bethke. New York: Touchstone, 1997.

Câmara, Hélder. *Correspondencia conciliar 1962–1965*. Obras Completas 1. Recife, 2004.

Carfora, Anna, and Sergio Tanzarella, *Il cristiano tra potere e mondanità. 15 gravi malattie secondo papa Francesco*. Trapani: Il Pozzo di Giacobbe, 2015.

Carta de apoio ao Papa Francisco. 2015. http://www.ihu.unisinos.br/noticias/548776-carta-de-apoio-ao-papa-francisco.

D'Ambrosio, Rocco. *Come pensano e agiscono le istituzioni*. Bologna: EDB, 2011.

———. *Il potere e chi lo detiene*. Bologna: EDB, 2011.

de Bortoli, Ferruccio. Intervista: "Benedetto XVI non è una statua; Partecipa alla vita della Chiesa." *Corriere della Sera*. March 5, 2014. http://www.corriere.it/cronache/14_marzo_04/vi -racconto-mio-primo-anno-papa-90f8a1c4-a3eb-11e3-b352 -9ec6f8a34ecc.shtml.

Douglas, Mary. *How Institutions Think*. Syracuse: Syracuse University Press, 1986.

"English Translation of Pope Francis' *Corriere della Sera* Interview." Zenit. March 5, 2014. https://zenit.org/articles /english-translation-of-pope-francis-corriere-della-sera -interview/.

Francis. Address to the Fifth National Convention of the Italian Church. November 10, 2015. http://w2.vatican.va/content /francesco/en/speeches/2015/november/documents/papa -francesco_20151110_firenze-convegno-chiesa-italiana.html.

———. Address to Journalists. March 16, 2013. https://zenit .org/articles/pope-francis-address-to-journalists/.

———. Address to Participants in the Convention Sponsored by the Congregation for the Clergy on the Fiftieth Anniversary of the Conciliar Decrees *Optatam Totius* and *Presbyterorum Ordinis*. November 20, 2015. https://w2.vatican.va/content /francesco/en/speeches/2015/november/documents/papa -francesco_20151120_formazione-sacerdoti.html.

———. Address to Participants in the Italian Conference of Major Superiors (CISM). November 7, 2014. http://m.vatican .va/content/francescomobile/en/speeches/2014/november /documents/papa-francesco_20141107_conferenza-italiana -superiori-maggiori.html.

———. Address to Participants in the Plenary of the Pontifical Council for Promoting the New Evangelization. October 14, 2014. https://w2.vatican.va/content/francesco/en/speeches /2013/october/documents/papa-francesco_20131014 _plenaria-consiglio-nuova-evangelizzazione.html.

————. Address to Pilgrims Celebrating Blessed Oscar Romero. October 30, 2015. Zenit translation. https://zenit.org/articles/pope-s-address-to-pilgrims-celebrating-blessed-oscar-romero/.

————. Address to the Delegates of the International Association of Penal Law. October 23, 2014. https://w2.vatican.va/content/francesco/en/speeches/2014/october/documents/papa-francesco_20141023_associazione-internazionale-diritto-penale.html.

————. Angelus. September 6, 2015. https://w2.vatican.va/content/francesco/en/angelus/2015/documents/papa-francesco_angelus_20150906.html.

————. Angelus. November 8, 2015. https://w2.vatican.va/content/francesco/en/angelus/2015/documents/papa-francesco_angelus_20151108.html.

————. Apostolic Exhortation *Evangelii Gaudium* (On the Proclamation of the Gospel in Today's World). November 24, 2013. http://w2.vatican.va/content/francesco/en/apost_exhortations/documents/papa-francesco_esortazione-ap_20131124_evangelii-gaudium.html.

————. Bull of Indiction of the Extraordinary Jubilee of Mercy *Misericordiae vultus*. April 11, 2015, n. 19. https://w2.vatican.va/content/francesco/en/apost_letters/documents/papa-francesco_bolla_20150411_misericordiae-vultus.html.

————. Encyclical letter *Laudato Sì* (On Care for Our Common Home). May 24, 2015, nos. 66, 70, 141. http://w2.vatican.va/content/francesco/en/encyclicals/documents/papa-francesco_20150524_enciclica-laudato-si.html.

————. General Audience. September 3, 2014. https://w2.vatican.va/content/francesco/en/audiences/2014/documents/papa-francesco_20140903_udienza-generale.html.

————. Holy Mass and Opening of the Holy Door. December 8, 2015. https://w2.vatican.va/content/francesco/en/homilies/2015/documents/papa-francesco_20151208_giubileo-omelia-apertura.html.

————. Holy Mass for the Marian Day on the Occasion of the Year of Faith. October 13, 2013. http://w2.vatican.va /content/francesco/en/homilies/2013/documents/papa -francesco_20131013_omelia-giornata-mariana.html.

————. Holy Mass on the Solemnity of the Epiphany of the Lord. January 6, 2016. https://w2.vatican.va/content/francesco /en/homilies/2016/documents/papa-francesco_20160106 _omelia-epifania.html.

————. First Greeting of the Holy Father Pope Francis. March 13, 2013. http://w2.vatican.va/content/francesco/en/speeches /2013/march/documents/papa-francesco_20130313 _benedizione-urbi-et-orbi.html.

————. In-Flight Press Conference from Mexico to Rome. February 17, 2016. https://w2.vatican.va/content/francesco /en/speeches/2016/february/documents/papa-francesco _20160217_messico-conferenza-stampa.html.

————. In-flight Press Conference from the Philippines to Rome. January 19, 2015. https://w2.vatican.va/content/francesco /en/speeches/2015/january/documents/papa-francesco _20150119_srilanka-filippine-conferenza-stampa.html.

————. Interview with Journalists during the Return Flight from the Holy Land. May 26, 2014. https://w2.vatican.va/content /francesco/en/speeches/2014/may/documents/papa -francesco_20140526_terra-santa-conferenza-stampa.html.

————. Meeting with the Bishops of the United States of America. September 23, 2015. https://w2.vatican.va/content /francesco/en/speeches/2015/september/documents/papa -francesco_20150923_usa-vescovi.html.

————. Meeting with the Participants in the Fifth Convention of the Italian Church. November 10, 2015. https://w2.vatican .va/content/francesco/en/speeches/2015/november /documents/papa-francesco_20151110_firenze-convegno -chiesa-italiana.html.

————. Meeting with the People and Various Social Categories of the Scampia Neighbourhood. March 21, 2015. https://w2 .vatican.va/content/francesco/en/speeches/2015/march

/documents/papa-francesco_20150321_napoli-pompei
-popolazione-scampia.html.

———. Meeting with the World of Culture. September
22, 2013. https://w2.vatican.va/content/francesco/en
/speeches/2013/september/documents/papa-francesco
_20130922_cultura-cagliari.html.

———. Meeting with the World of Labour and Industry.
July 5, 2014. https://w2.vatican.va/content/francesco/en
/speeches/2014/july/documents/papa-francesco_20140705
_molise-mondo-del-lavoro.html.

———. Meeting with the Young People. November 27, 2015.
https://w2.vatican.va/content/francesco/en/speeches
/2015/november/documents/papa-francesco_20151127
_kenya-giovani.html.

———. Message to the Italian Catholic University Federation
(FUCI). October 14, 2014. https://zenit.org/articles/pope
-s-address-to-university-students-federation/.

———. Morning Meditation in the Chapel of *Domus Sanctae Marthae.*
April 19, 2013. http://w2.vatican.va/content/francesco/it
/cotidie/2013/documents/papa-francesco-cotidie
_20130419_contro-ideologia.html.

———. Morning Mediation in the Chapel of the *Domus Sanctae
Marthae.* June 16, 2014. https://w2.vatican.va/content
/francesco/en/cotidie/2014/documents/papa-francesco
-cotidie_20140616_price-corruption.html.

———. Morning Meditation in the Chapel of *Domus Sanctae
Marthae.* November 11, 2013. https://w2.vatican.va/content
/francesco/en/cotidie/2013/documents/papa-francesco
-cotidie_20131111_sinners-yes.html.

———. Papal Mass for the Repose of the Souls of the Cardinals
and Bishops who Died over the Course of the Year. November 3,
2015. https://w2.vatican.va/content/francesco/en/homilies
/2015/documents/papa-francesco_20151103_omelia
-suffra gio-defunti.html.

———. Presentation of Christmas Greetings to the Roman Curia.
December 22, 2014. https://w2.vatican.va/content/francesco

/en/speeches/2014/december/documents/papa-francesco
_20141222_curia-romana.html.

———. Presentation of the Christmas Greetings to the Roman
Curia. December 21, 2015. https://w2.vatican.va/content
/francesco/en/speeches/2015/december/documents/papa
-francesco_20151221_curia-romana.html.

———. Press Conference during the Return Flight from Rio De
Janeiro for World Youth Day XXVIII. July 28, 2013. http://
w2.vatican.va/content/francesco/en/speeches/2013/july
/documents/papa-francesco_20130728_gmg-conferenza
-stampa.html.

———. *The Name of God Is Mercy: A Conversation with Andrea
Tornielli.* Translated by Oonagh Stransky. New York: Random
House, 2016.

———. Vespers with Priests and Religious. September 24,
2015. http://w2.vatican.va/content/francesco/en/homilies
/2015/documents/papa-francesco_20150924_usa-omelia
-vespri-nyc.html.

———. Video-Message to Participants in the Initiative Entitled "Ten Squares for Ten Commandments." June 8, 2013.
https://w2.vatican.va/content/francesco/en/messages
/pont-messages/2013/documents/papa-francesco_20130608
_videomessaggio-10piazze.html.

Guardini, Romano. *Briefe über Selbstbildung.* Mainz: Grünewald,
1985.

Guitton, Jean. *Le Christ de ma vie. Dialogue avec Jean Dorè.* Paris:
Desclee, 1987.

John Paul II. Encyclical Letter *Centesimus Annus* (On the
Hundredth Anniversary of *Rerum Novarum*). May 1, 1991.
http://w2.vatican.va/content/john-paul-ii/en/encyclicals
/documents/hf_jp-ii_enc_01051991_centesimus-annus.html.

———. Encyclical Letter *Redemptor Hominis.* March 4, 1979.
http://w2.vatican.va/content/john-paul-ii/en/encyclicals
/documents/hf_jp-ii_enc_04031979_redemptor-hominis
.html.

————. Encyclical Letter *Sollicitudo Rei Socialis* (On the Twentieth Anniversary of *Populorum Progressio*). December 30, 1987, n. 37. http://w2.vatican.va/content/john-paul-ii/en/encyclicals /documents/hf_jp-ii_enc_30121987_sollicitudo-rei-socialis .html.

Jung, Carl. *Aion*. Vol. 9, bk. 2, of *Collected Works* of C. G. Jung. Princeton, NJ: Princeton University Press, 1979.

————. "On the Psychology of the Unconscious." In *Two Essays on Analytical Psychology*. Vol. 7 of *Collected Works of C. G. Jung*. Princeton, NJ: Princeton University Press, 1972.

Kets de Vries, Manfred F. R. *Leaders, Fools and Impostors: Essays on the Psychology of Leadership*. San Francisco: Jossey-Bass, 1993.

La Valle, Raniero. *Chi sono io Francesco? Cronache di cose mai viste*. Firenze: Ponte delle Grazie, 2015.

Maccise, Camilo. "Violence in the Church." *The Tablet* (November 22, 2003): 8–9.

Magrassi, Mariano. *Vivere la Chiesa*. Vol. 1. Noci: Edizioni La Scala, 1988.

Mazzolari, Primo. *La pieve sull'argine*. Bologna: EDB, 1978.

Merini, Alda. *Fiore di poesia: 1951–1997*. Torino: Einaudi, 1998.

Mignozzi, Vito. *Come un sacramento. Uno stile per essere Chiesa oggi*. Todi: Tau, 2011.

Milani, Lorenzo. *Esperienze pastorali*. Firenze: Lef, 1957.

Mounier, Emmanual. *The Character of Man*. Translated by Cynthia Rowland. New York: Harper & Brothers, 1956.

Nicodemo, E. "Nota redazionale: Il ritorno dell'arcivescovo dal Concilio." In *L'Odegitria: Bollettino Ecclesiastico ufficiale per l'Archidiocesi di Bari*. 1965.

Paul VI. Encyclical *Ecclesiam Suam* (On the Church). August 6, 1964. http://w2.vatican.va/content/paul-vi/en/encyclicals /documents/hf_p-vi_enc_06081964_ecclesiam.html.

————. Encyclical *Populorum Progressio* (On the Development of Peoples). March 26, 1967. http://w2.vatican.va/content /paul-vi/en/encyclicals/documents/hf_p-vi_enc_26031967 _populorum.html.

Scalfari, Eugenio. "The Pope: How the Church Will Change." *La Repubblica*. October 1, 2013. http://www.repubblica.it /cultura/2013/10/01/news/pope_s_conversation_with _scalfari_english-67643118/?refresh_ce.

Second Vatican Council. *Lumen Gentium* (Dogmatic Constitution on the Church). November 21, 1964, n. 1. In *Vatican Council II: Constitutions, Decrees, Declarations*, edited by Austin Flannery. Collegeville, MN: Liturgical Press, 2014.

―――. *Gaudium et Spes* (Pastoral Constitution on the Church in the Modern World). December 7, 1965, n. 76. In *Vatican Council II: Constitutions, Decrees, Declarations*, edited by Austin Flannery. Collegeville, MN: Liturgical Press, 2014.

William Shakespeare. *Henry IV*, part 2.

Spadaro, Antonio. "Interview with Pope Francis." https:// w2.vatican.va/content/francesco/en/speeches/2013 /september/documents/papa-francesco_20130921_intervista -spadaro.html.

Thomas Aquinas. *Summa Theologica.* New York: Benziger Brothers, 1947.

Ventura, Marco. *Creduli e credenti. Il declino di Stato e Chiesa come questione di fede*. Torino: Einaudi, 2014.

Voegelin, Eric. *Autobiographical Reflections.* Columbia: University of Missouri Press, 2006.

―――. *The Nature of Law and Related Legal Writings*. Edited by Robert Anthony Pascal, James Lee Babin, and John William Corrington. Baton Rouge: Louisiana State University Press, 1991.

"We Need to Fight for a World without Poverty." INSP News Service. November 27, 2015. http://insp.ngo/exclusive -pope-francis-interview-for-street-papers/.

Yanez, H. M., ed. *Evangelii gaudium: il testo ci interroga. Chiavi di lettura e prospettive*. Rome: Gregorian & Biblical Press, 2015.